Lab Manual

Module K

HOLT McDOUGAL

HOUGHTON MIFFLIN HARCOURT

Acknowledgements for Covers

Cover Photo Credits

Micro-circuit board (bg) ©Roger Du Buisson/Corbis; *tweezer* (l) ©Corbis; *bulbs* (cl) ©Peter Gridley/Photographer's Choice RF/Getty Images; *wind tunnel* (cr) ©George Steinmetz/Corbis; *bioscience* (r) ©Andrew Brookes/Corbis

Printed in the U.S.A.

ISBN 978-0-547-59267-1

4 5 6 7 8 9 10 0982 20 19 18 17 16 15 14 13 12
4500378440 A B C D E F G

Contents

INTRODUCTION

TEACHER LAB SAFETY

STUDENT LAB SAFETY

Unit 1 The Nature of Science

Unit 2 Measurement and Data

Unit 3 Engineering, Technology, and Society

Using Your *ScienceFusion* Lab Program

Your *ScienceFusion* Lab Program is designed to include activities that address a variety of student levels, inquiry levels, time availability, and materials. In this Lab Manual, you will find that each student activity is preceded by Teacher Resources with valuable information about the activity.

Activity Type: Quick Lab

Each lesson within each unit is supported by two to three short activities called Quick Labs. Quick Labs involve simple materials and set-up. The student portion of each Quick Lab should take less than 30 minutes. Each Quick Lab includes Teacher Resources and one Student Datasheet.

Activity Types: Exploration Lab, Field Lab, and S.T.E.M. Lab

Each unit is supported by one to four additional labs that require one or more class periods to complete. Each Exploration, Field, and S.T.E.M. Lab includes Teacher Resources and two Student Datasheets. Each Student Datasheet is targeted to address different inquiry levels. Below is a description of each lab:

- **Exploration Labs** are traditional lab activities. The labs are designed to be conducted with standard laboratory equipment and materials.
- **Field Labs** are lab activities that are partially or completely performed outside the classroom or laboratory.
- **S.T.E.M. Labs** are lab activities that focus on Science, Technology, Engineering, and Math skills.

Inquiry Level

The inquiry level of each activity indicates the level at which students direct the activity. An activity that is entirely student-directed is often called Open Inquiry or Independent Inquiry. True Open or Independent Inquiry is based on a question posed by students, uses experimental processes designed by students, and requires students to find the connections between data and content. These types of activities result from student interest in the world around them. The *ScienceFusion* Lab Program provides activities that allow for a wide variety of student involvement.

- DIRECTED Inquiry is the least student-directed of the inquiry levels. Directed Inquiry activities provide students with an introduction to content, a procedure to follow, and direction on how to organize and analyze data.
- GUIDED Inquiry indicates that an activity is moderately student-directed. Guided Inquiry activities require students to select materials, procedural steps, data analysis techniques, or other aspects of the activity.
- INDEPENDENT Inquiry indicates that an activity is highly student-directed. Though students are provided with ideas, partial procedures, or suggestions, they are responsible for selecting many aspects of the activity.

Each Quick Lab includes one Student Datasheet that is written to support the inquiry level indicated on the Teacher Resources. Each Exploration Lab, Field Lab, and S.T.E.M. Lab includes two Student Datasheets, each written to support an inquiry level. In addition, the Teacher Resources includes one or more modification suggestions to adjust the inquiry level.

Student Level

The *ScienceFusion* Lab Program is designed to provide successful experiences for all levels of students.

- BASIC activities focus on introductory content and concepts taught in the lesson. These activities can be used with any level of student, including those who may have learning or language difficulties, but they may not provide a challenge for advanced students.
- GENERAL activities are appropriate for most students.
- ADVANCED activities require good understanding of the content and concepts in the lesson or ask students to manipulate content to arrive at the learning objective. Advanced activities may provide a challenge to advanced students, but they may be difficult for average or basic-level students.

Lab Ratings

Each activity is rated on three criteria to provide you with information that you may find useful when determining if an activity is appropriate for your resources.

- **Teacher Prep** rating indicates the amount of preparation you will need to provide before students can perform the activity.
- **Student Setup** rating indicates the amount of preparation students will need to perform before they begin to collect data.
- **Cleanup** rating indicates the amount of effort required to dispose of materials and disassemble the set-up of the activity.

Teacher Notes

Information and background that may be helpful to you can be found in the Teacher Notes section of the Teacher Resources. The information includes hints and a list of skills that students will practice during the activity.

Science Kit

Hands-on materials needed to complete all the labs in the Lab Manual for each module have been conveniently configured into consumable and non-consumable kits. Common materials provided by parents or your school/district are not included in the kits. Laboratory equipment commonly found in most schools has been separately packaged in a Grades 6–8 Inquiry Equipment Kit. This economical option allows schools to buy equipment only if they need it and can be shared among teachers and across grade levels. For more information on the material kits or to order, contact your local Holt McDougal sales representative or call customer service at 800-462-6595.

Online Lab Resources

The *ScienceFusion* Lab Program offers many additional resources online through our web site thinkcentral.com. These resources include:

Teacher Notes, Transparencies, and **Copymasters** are found in the Online Toolkit. Student-friendly tutorial Transparencies are available to print as transparencies or handouts. Each set of Transparencies is supported by Teacher Notes that include background information, teaching tips, and techniques. Teacher Notes, Transparencies, and Copymatsters are available to teach a broad range of skills.

- **Modeling Experimental Design** Teacher Notes and Transparencies cover Scientific Methods skills, such as Making Qualitative Observations, Developing a Hypothesis, and Making Valid Inferences.

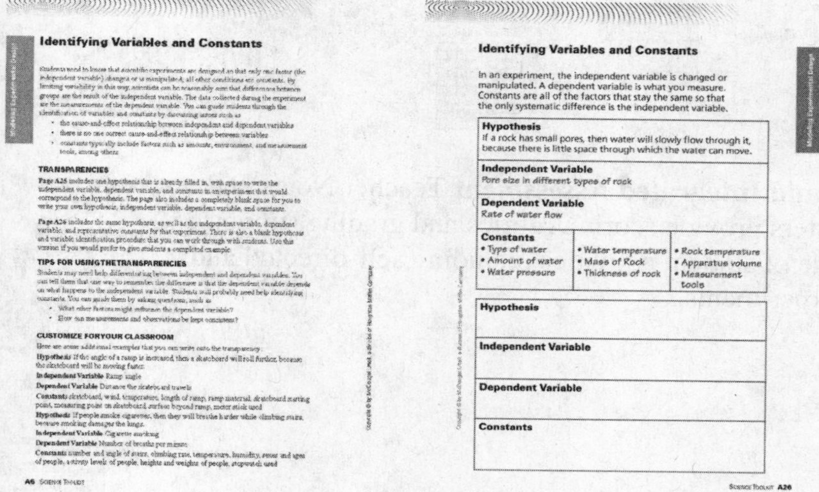

Identifying Variables and Constants

Students need to know that scientific experiments are designed so that only one factor (the independent variable) changes or is manipulated; all other conditions are constants. By limiting variability in this way, scientists can be reasonably sure that differences between groups are the result of the independent variable. The data collected during the experiment are the measurements of the dependent variable. You can guide students through the identification of variables and constants by discussing issues such as

- the cause-and-effect relationship between independent and dependent variables
- there is no one correct cause-and-effect relationship between variables
- constants typically include factors such as amounts, environment, and measurement tools, among others

TRANSPARENCIES

Page A25 includes one hypothesis that is already filled in, with space to write the independent variable, dependent variable, and constants in an experiment that would correspond to the hypothesis. The page also includes a completely blank space for you to write your own hypothesis, independent variable, dependent variable, and constants.

Page A26 includes the same hypothesis, as well as the independent variable, dependent variable, and representative constants for that experiment. There is also a blank hypothesis and variable identification procedure that you can work through with students. Use this version if you would prefer to give students a completed example.

TIPS FOR USING THE TRANSPARENCIES

Students may need help differentiating between independent and dependent variables. You can tell them that one way to remember the difference is that the dependent variable depends on what happens to the independent variable. Students will probably need help identifying constants. You can guide them by asking questions, such as

- What other factors might influence the dependent variable?
- How can measurements and observations be kept consistent?

CUSTOMIZE FOR YOUR CLASSROOM

Here are some additional examples that you can write onto the transparency.

Hypothesis If the angle of a ramp is increased, then a skateboard will roll farther, because the skateboard will be moving faster.

Independent Variable Ramp angle

Dependent Variable Distance the skateboard travels

Constants skateboard, wind, temperature, length of ramp, ramp material, skateboard starting point, measuring point on skateboard, surface beyond ramp, meter stick used

Hypothesis If people smoke cigarettes, then they will breathe harder while climbing stairs, because smoking damages the lungs.

Independent Variable Cigarette smoking

Dependent Variable Number of breaths per minute

Constants number and angle of stairs, climbing rate, temperature, humidity, sexes and ages of people, activity levels of people, heights and weights of people, stopwatch used

A6 Science Toolkit

Identifying Variables and Constants

In an experiment, the independent variable is changed or manipulated. A dependent variable is what you measure. Constants are all of the factors that stay the same so that the only systematic difference is the independent variable.

Hypothesis *If a rock has small pores, then water will slowly flow through it, because there is little space through which the water can move.*		
Independent Variable *Pore size in different types of rock*		
Dependent Variable *Rate of water flow*		
Constants • *Type of water* • *Amount of water* • *Water pressure*	• *Water temperature* • *Mass of Rock* • *Thickness of rock*	• *Rock temperature* • *Apparatus volume* • *Measurement tools*

Hypothesis
Independent Variable
Dependent Variable
Constants

Science Toolkit A26

- **Writing in the Sciences** Teacher Notes and Transparencies teach written communication skills, such as Writing a Lab Report and Maintaining a Science Notebook. In addition, the Lab Report Template provides a structured format that students can use as the basis for their own lab reports.

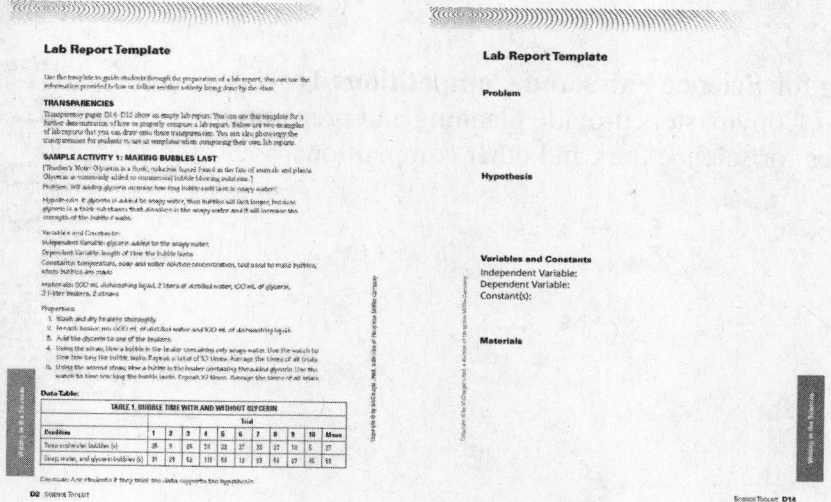

Lab Report Template

Use the template to guide students through the preparation of a lab report. You can use the information provided below or follow another activity being done by the class.

TRANSPARENCIES

Transparency pages D14–D15 show an empty lab report. You can use this template for a further demonstration of how to properly compose a lab report. Below are two examples of lab reports that you can draw onto these transparencies. You can also photocopy the transparencies for students to use as templates when composing their own lab reports.

SAMPLE ACTIVITY 1: MAKING BUBBLES LAST

Data Table:

TABLE 1. BUBBLE TIME WITH AND WITHOUT GLYCERIN											
	Trial										
Condition	1	2	3	4	5	6	7	8	9	10	Mean
Soap and water bubbles (s)	[illegible]	[illegible]	[illegible]	[illegible]	[illegible]	[illegible]	[illegible]	[illegible]	[illegible]	[illegible]	[illegible]
Soap, water, and glycerin bubbles (s)	[illegible]	[illegible]	[illegible]	[illegible]	[illegible]	[illegible]	[illegible]	[illegible]	[illegible]	[illegible]	[illegible]

D2 Science Toolkit

Lab Report Template

Problem

Hypothesis

Variables and Constants
Independent Variable:
Dependent Variable:
Constant(s):

Materials

Science Toolkit D14

- **Math in Science Tools** Teacher Notes and Transparencies teach the math skills that are needed for data analysis in labs. These Teacher Notes and Transparencies support the S.T.E.M. concepts found throughout the *ScienceFusion* program.

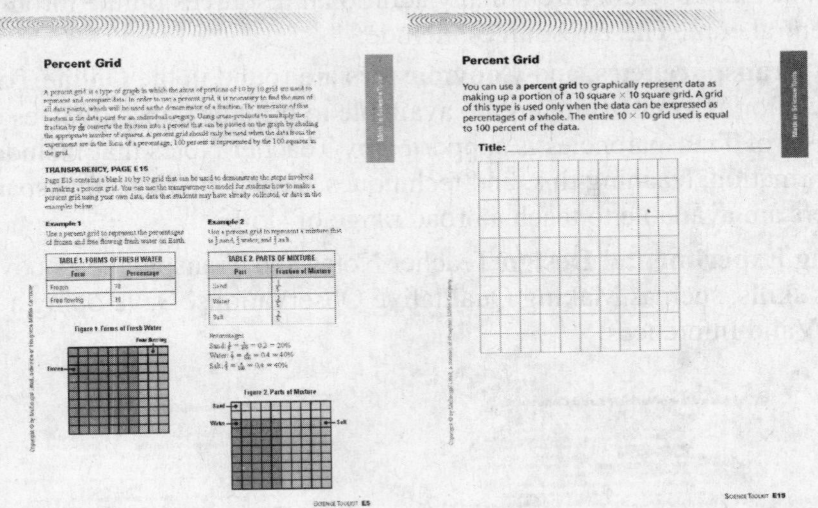

Percent Grid

A percent grid is a type of graph in which the sizes of portions of 10 by 10 grid are used to represent and compare data. In order to use a percent grid, it is necessary to find the sum of all data points, which will be used as the denominator of a fraction. The numerator of this fraction is the data point for an individual category. Using cross-products to multiply the fraction by $\frac{100}{100}$ converts the fraction into a percent that can be plotted on the graph by shading the appropriate number of squares. A percent grid should only be used when the data from the experiment are in the form of a percentage; 100 percent is represented by the 100 squares in the grid.

TRANSPARENCY, PAGE E15

Page E15 contains a blank 10 by 10 grid that can be used to demonstrate the steps involved in making a percent grid. You can use the transparency to model for students how to make a percent grid using your own data, data that students may have already collected, or data in the examples below.

Example 1

Use a percent grid to represent the percentages of frozen and free flowing fresh water on Earth.

TABLE 1. FORMS OF FRESH WATER	
Form	Percentage
Frozen	[illegible]
Free flowing	[illegible]

Figure 1. Forms of Fresh Water

Example 2

Use a percent grid to represent a mixture that is $\frac{1}{5}$ sand, $\frac{2}{5}$ water, and $\frac{2}{5}$ salt.

TABLE 2. PARTS OF MIXTURE	
Part	Fraction of Mixture
Sand	$\frac{1}{5}$
Water	$\frac{2}{5}$
Salt	$\frac{2}{5}$

Percentages:
Sand: $\frac{1}{5} = \frac{20}{100} = 0.2 = 20\%$
Water: $\frac{2}{5} = \frac{40}{100} = 0.4 = 40\%$
Salt: $\frac{2}{5} = \frac{40}{100} = 0.4 = 40\%$

Figure 2. Parts of Mixture

SCIENCE TOOLKIT E5

Percent Grid

You can use a **percent grid** to graphically represent data as making up a portion of a 10 square × 10 square grid. A grid of this type is used only when the data can be expressed as percentages of a whole. The entire 10 × 10 grid used is equal to 100 percent of the data.

Title: ______________________

SCIENCE TOOLKIT E15

- **Rubrics and Integrated Assessment** Teacher Notes and Copymasters provide scoring rubrics and grading support for a range of student activities including self-directed and guided experiments.

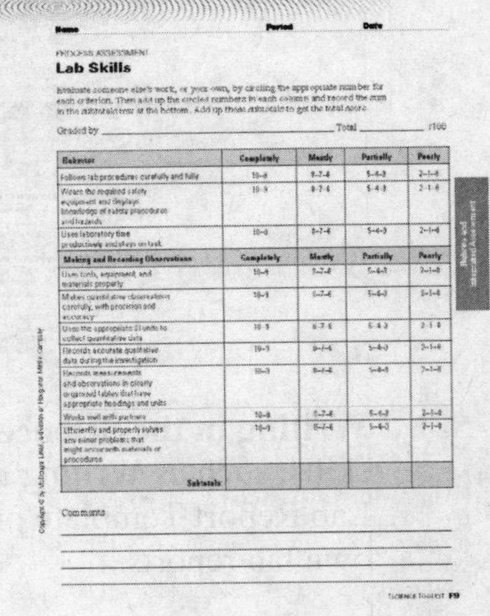

Name ______ Period ______ Date ______

PROCESS ASSESSMENT

Lab Skills

Evaluate someone else's work, or your own, by circling the appropriate number for each criterion. Then add up the circled numbers in each column and record the sum in the subtotals row at the bottom. Add up these subtotals to get the total score.

Graded by ______________________ Total ________ /100

Behavior	Completely	Mostly	Partially	Poorly
Follows lab procedures carefully and fully	10–9	8–7–6	5–4–3	2–1–0
Wears the required safety equipment and displays knowledge of safety procedures and hazards	10–9	8–7–6	5–4–3	2–1–0
Uses laboratory time productively and stays on task	10–9	8–7–6	5–4–3	2–1–0
Making and Recording Observations	**Completely**	**Mostly**	**Partially**	**Poorly**
Uses tools, equipment, and materials properly	10–9	8–7–6	5–4–3	2–1–0
Makes quantitative observations carefully, with precision and accuracy	10–9	8–7–6	5–4–3	2–1–0
Uses the appropriate SI units to collect quantitative data	10–9	8–7–6	5–4–3	2–1–0
Records accurate qualitative data during the investigation	10–9	8–7–6	5–4–3	2–1–0
Records measurements and observations in clearly organized tables that have appropriate headings and units	10–9	8–7–6	5–4–3	2–1–0
Works well with partners	10–9	8–7–6	5–4–3	2–1–0
Efficiently and properly solves any minor problems that might occur with materials or procedures	10–9	8–7–6	5–4–3	2–1–0
Subtotals				

Comments

SCIENCE TOOLKIT F9

- **Planning for Science Fairs and Competitions** Teacher Notes and Copymasters provide planning and preparation techniques for science fairs and other competitions.

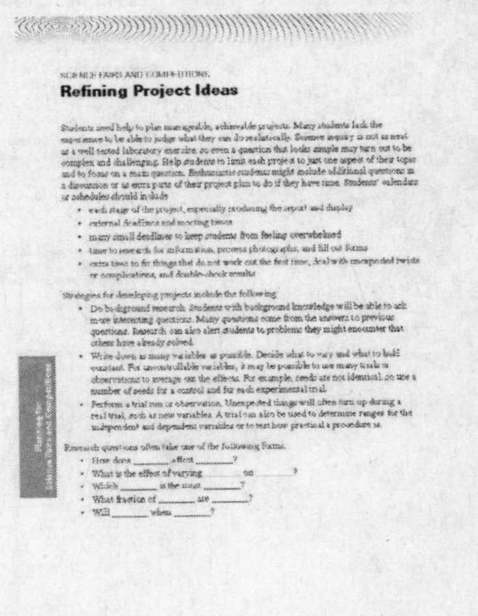

SCIENCE FAIRS AND COMPETITIONS

Refining Project Ideas

Students need help to plan manageable, achievable projects. Many students lack the experience to be able to judge what they can do realistically. Science inquiry is not as neat as a well tested laboratory exercise, so even a question that looks simple may turn out to be complex and challenging. Help students to limit each project to just one aspect of their topic and to focus on a main question. Enthusiastic students might include additional questions in a discussion or as extra parts of their project plan to do if they have time. Students' calendars or schedules should include

- each stage of the project, especially producing the report and display
- external deadlines and meeting times
- many small deadlines to keep students from feeling overwhelmed
- time to research for information, process photographs, and fill out forms
- extra time to fix things that do not work out the first time, deal with unexpected twists or complications, and double-check results

Strategies for developing projects include the following:

- Do background research. Students with background knowledge will be able to ask more interesting questions. Many questions come from the answers to previous questions. Research can also alert students to problems they might encounter that others have already solved.
- Write down as many variables as possible. Decide what to vary and what to hold constant. For uncontrollable variables, it may be possible to use many trials or observations to average out the effects. For example, seeds are not identical, so use a number of seeds for a control and for each experimental trial.
- Perform a trial run or observation. Unexpected things will often turn up during a real trial, such as new variables. A trial can also be used to determine ranges for the independent and dependent variables or to test how practical a procedure is.

Research questions often take one of the following forms:

- How does ______ affect ______?
- What is the effect of varying ______ on ______?
- Which ______ is the most ______?
- What fraction of ______ are ______?
- Will ______ when ______?

K2 SCIENCE TOOLKIT

Making Your Laboratory a Safe Place

Concern for safety must begin before any activity in the classroom and before students enter the lab. A careful review of the facilities should be a basic part of preparation for each school term. You should investigate the physical environment, identify any safety risks, and inspect your work areas for compliance with safety regulations.

The review of the lab should be thorough, and all safety issues must be addressed immediately. Keep a file of your review, and add to the list each year. This will allow you to continue to raise the standard of safety in your lab and classroom.

Many classroom experiments, demonstrations, and other activities are classics that have been used for years. This familiarity may lead to a comfort that can obscure inherent safety concerns. Review all experiments, demonstrations, and activities for safety concerns before presenting them to the class. Identify and eliminate potential safety hazards.

1. **Identify the Risks** Before introducing any activity, demonstration, or experiment to the class, analyze it and consider what could possibly go wrong. Carefully review the list of materials to make sure they are safe. Inspect the equipment in your lab or classroom to make sure it is in good working order. Read the procedures to make sure they are safe. Record any hazards or concerns you identify.
2. **Evaluate the Risks** Minimize the risks you identified in the last step without sacrificing learning. Remember that no activity you perform in the lab or classroom is worth risking injury. Thus, extremely hazardous activities, or those that violate your school's policies, must be eliminated. For activities that present smaller risks, analyze each risk carefully to determine its likelihood. If the pedagogical value of the activity does not outweigh the risks, the activity must be eliminated.
3. **Select Controls to Address Risks** Even low-risk activities require controls to eliminate or minimize the risks. Make sure that in devising controls you do not substitute an equally or more hazardous alternative. Some control methods include the following:
   - Explicit verbal and written warnings may be added or posted.
   - Equipment may be rebuilt or relocated, parts may be replaced, or equipment be replaced entirely by safer alternatives.
   - Risky procedures may be eliminated.
   - Activities may be changed from student activities to teacher demonstrations.
4. **Implement and Review Selected Controls** Controls do not help if they are forgotten or not enforced. The implementation and review of controls should be as systematic and thorough as the initial analysis of safety concerns in the lab and laboratory activities.

Safety with Chemicals

Label student reagent containers with the substance's name and hazard class(es) (flammable, reactive, etc.). Dispose of hazardous waste chemicals according to federal, state, and local regulations. Refer to the MSDS for recommended disposal procedures. Remove all sources of flames, sparks, and heat from the laboratory when any flammable material is being used.

Material Safety Data Sheets

The purpose of a Material Safety Data Sheet (MSDS) is to provide readily accessible information on chemical substances commonly used in the science laboratory or in industry. The MSDS should be kept on file and referred to BEFORE handling ANY chemical. The MSDS can also be used to instruct students on chemical hazards, to evaluate spill and disposal procedures, and to warn of incompatibility with other chemicals or mixtures.

Storing Chemicals

Never store chemicals alphabetically, as this greatly increases the risk of promoting a violent reaction.

Storage Suggestions

1. Always lock the storeroom and all its cabinets when not in use.
2. Students should not be allowed in the storeroom and preparation area.
3. Avoid storing chemicals on the floor of the storeroom.
4. Do not store chemicals above eye level or on the top shelf in the storeroom.
5. Be sure shelf assemblies are firmly secured to the walls.
6. Provide anti-roll lips on all shelves.
7. Shelving should be constructed out of wood. Metal cabinets and shelves are easily corroded.
8. Avoid metal, adjustable shelf supports and clips. They can corrode, causing shelves to collapse.
9. Acids, flammables, poisons, and oxidizers should each be stored in their own locking storage cabinet.

Safety with Animals

It is recommended that teachers follow the NABT Position Statement "The Use of Animals in Biology Education" issued by the National Association of Biology Teachers (available at www.nabt.org).

Safety In Handling Preserved Materials

The following practices are recommended when handling preserved specimens:

1. NEVER dissect road-kills or nonpreserved slaughterhouse materials.
2. Wear protective gloves and splash-proof safety goggles at all times when handling preserving fluids and preserved specimens and during dissection.
3. Wear lab aprons. Use of an old shirt or smock under the lab apron is recommended.
4. Conduct dissection activities in a well-ventilated area.
5. Do not allow preservation or body-cavity fluids to contact skin. Fixatives do not distinguish between living or dead tissues. Biological supply firms may use formalin-based fixatives of varying concentrations to initially fix zoological and botanical specimens. Some provide specimens that are freezedried and rehydrated in a 10% isopropyl alcohol solution. Many suppliers provide fixed botanical materials in 50% glycerin.

Reduction Of Free Formaldehyde

Currently, federal regulations mandate a permissible exposure level of 0.75 ppm for formaldehyde. Contact your supplier for Material Data Safety Sheet (MSDS) that details the amount of formaldehyde present as well as gas-emitting characteristics for individual specimens. Prewash specimens (in a loosely covered container) in running tap water for 1–4 hours to dilute the fixative. Formaldehyde may also be chemically bound (thereby reducing danger) by immersing washed specimens in a 0.5–1.0% potassium bisulfate solution overnight or by placing them in 1% phenoxyethanol holding solutions.

Safety with Microbes

WHAT YOU CAN'T SEE CAN HURT YOU

Pathogenic (disease-causing) microorganisms are not appropriate investigation tools in the high school laboratory and should never be used.

Consult with the school nurse to screen students whose immune systems may be compromised by illness or who may be receiving immunosuppressive drug therapy. Such individuals are extraordinarily sensitive to potential infection from generally harmless microorganisms and should not participate in laboratory activities unless permitted to do so by a physician. Do not allow students who have any open cuts, abrasions, or open sores to work with microorganisms.

HOW TO USE ASEPTIC TECHNIQUE

- Demonstrate correct aseptic technique to students prior to conducting a lab activity. Never pipet liquid media by mouth. When possible, use sterile cotton applicator sticks instead of inoculating loops and Bunsen burner flames for culture inoculation. Remember to use appropriate precautions when disposing of cotton applicator sticks: they should be autoclaved or sterilized before disposal.
- Treat all microbes as pathogenic. Seal with tape all petri dishes containing bacterial cultures. Do not use blood agar plates, and never attempt to cultivate microbes from a human or animal source.
- Never dispose of microbe cultures without sterilizing them first. Autoclave or steam-sterilize at 120°C and 15 psi for 15 to 20 minutes all used cultures and any materials that have come in contact with them. If these devices are not available, flood or immerse these articles in full-strength household bleach for 30 minutes, and then discard. Use the autoclave or steam sterilizer yourself; do not allow students to use these devices.
- Wash all lab surfaces with a disinfectant solution before and after handling bacterial cultures.

HOW TO HANDLE BACTERIOLOGICAL SPILLS

- Never allow students to clean up bacteriological spills. Keep on hand a spill kit containing 500 mL of full-strength household bleach, biohazard bags (autoclavable), forceps, and paper towels.
- In the event of a bacterial spill, cover the area with a layer of paper towels. Wet the paper towels with bleach, and allow them to stand for 15 to 20 minutes. Wearing gloves and using forceps, place the residue in the biohazard bag. If broken glass is present, use a brush and dustpan to collect material, and place it in a suitably marked puncture-resistant container for disposal.

Personal Protective Equipment

Chemical goggles (Meeting ANSI Standard Z87.1) These should be worn with any chemical or chemical solution other than water, when heating substances, using any mechanical device, or observing physical processes that could eject an object.

Face shield (Meeting ANSI Standard Z87.1) Use in combination with eye goggles when working with corrosives.

Contact lenses The wearing of contact lenses for cosmetic reasons should be prohibited in the laboratory. If a student must wear contact lenses prescribed by a physician, that student should be instructed to wear eye-cup safety goggles, similar to swimmer's cup goggles, meeting ANSI Standard Z87.1.

Eye-wash station The device must be capable of delivering a copious, gentle flow of water to both eyes for at least 15 minutes. Portable liquid supply devices are not satisfactory and should not be used. A plumbed-in fixture or a perforated spray head on the end of a hose attached to a plumbed-in outlet is suitable if it is designed for use as an eye-wash fountain and meets ANSI Standard Z358.1. It must be within a 30-second walking distance from any spot in the room.

Safety shower (Meeting ANSI Standard Z358.1) Location should be within a 30-second walking distance from any spot in the room. Students should be instructed in the use of the safety shower in the event of a fire or chemical splash on their body that cannot simply be washed off.

Gloves Polyethylene, neoprene rubber, or disposable plastic may be used. Nitrile or butyl rubber gloves are recommended when handling corrosives.

Apron Rubber-coated cloth or vinyl (nylon-coated) halter is recommended.

Student Safety in the Laboratory

Systematic, careful lab work is an essential part of any science program. The equipment and apparatus students will use present various safety hazards. You must be aware of these hazards before students engage in any lab activity. The Teacher Resource Pages at the beginning of each lab in this Lab Manual will guide you in properly directing the equipment use during the experiments. Photocopy the information on the following pages for students. These safety rules always apply in the lab and in the field.

Name ______________________ Class ______________________ Date ______________

Safety Symbols

The following safety symbols will appear in the instructions for labs and activities to emphasize important notes of caution. Learn what they represent so that you can take the appropriate precautions.

	**Eye Protection** • Wear approved safety goggles at all times in the lab as directed. • If chemicals get into your eyes, flush your eyes immediately. • Do not wear contact lenses in the lab. • Do not look directly at the sun or any intense light source or laser.
	**Hand Safety** • Do not cut an object while holding the object in your hand. • Wear appropriate protective gloves when working with an open flame, chemicals, solutions, or wild or unknown plants. • Use a heat-resistant mitt to handle equipment that may be hot.
	**Clothing Protection** • Wear an apron or lab coat at all times in the lab. • Tie back long hair, secure loose clothing, and remove loose jewelry so that they do not knock over equipment, get caught in moving parts, or come into contact with hazardous materials or electrical connections. • Do not wear open-toed shoes, sandals, or canvas shoes in the lab. • When outside for lab, wear long sleeves, long pants, socks, and closed shoes.
	**Glassware Safety** • Inspect glassware before use; do not use chipped or cracked glassware. • Use heat-resistant glassware for heating materials or storing hot liquids. • Notify your teacher immediately if a piece of glassware or a light bulb breaks.
	**Sharp-Object Safety** • Use extreme care when handling all sharp and pointed instruments. • Cut objects on a suitable surface, always in a direction away from your body. • Be aware of sharp objects or edges on equipment or apparatus.
	**Chemical Safety** • If a chemical gets on your skin, on your clothing, or in your eyes, rinse it immediately (shower, faucet or eyewash fountain) and alert your teacher. • Do not clean up spilled chemicals yourself unless your teacher directs you to do so. • Do not inhale any gas or vapor unless your teacher directs you to do so. • Handle materials that emit vapors or gases in a well-ventilated area.

Name ____________________ Class ____________ Date ____________

Safety Symbols continued

Electrical Safety

- Do not use equipment with frayed electrical cords or loose plugs.
- Fasten electrical cords to work surfaces by using tape.
- Do not use electrical equipment near water or when clothing or hands are wet.
- Hold the plug housing when you plug in or unplug equipment.
- Be aware that wire coils in electrical circuits may heat up rapidly.

Heating Safety

- Be aware of any source of flames, sparks, or heat (such as open flames, heating coils, or hot plates) before working with any flammable substances.
- Avoid using open flames.

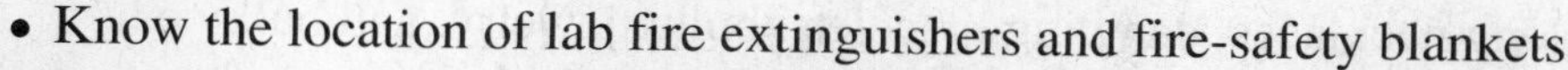

- Know the location of lab fire extinguishers and fire-safety blankets.
- Know your school's fire-evacuation routes.
- If your clothing catches on fire, walk to the lab shower to put out the fire.
- Never leave a hot plate unattended while it is turned on or while it is cooling.
- Use tongs or appropriate insulated holders when handling heated objects.
- Allow all equipment to cool before storing it.

Plant Safety

- Do not eat any part of a plant or plant seed.
- When outside, do not pick any wild plants unless your teacher instructs you to do so.
- Wash your hands thoroughly after handling any part of a plant.

Animal Safety

- Handle animals only as your teacher directs.
- Treat animals carefully and respectfully.
- Wash your hands thoroughly after handling any animal.

Proper Waste Disposal

- Clean and sanitize all work surfaces and personal protective equipment after each lab period as directed by your teacher.
- Dispose of hazardous materials only as directed by your teacher.
- Dispose of sharp objects (such as broken glass) in the appropriate sharps or broken glass container as directed by your teacher.

Hygienic Care

- Keep your hands away from your face while you are working on any activity.
- Wash your hands thoroughly before you leave the lab or after any activity.
- Remove contaminated clothing immediately.

Name ______________________ Class ______________ Date ______________

Safety in the Laboratory

1. **Always wear a lab apron and safety goggles.** Wear these safety devices whenever you are in the lab, not just when you are working on an experiment.
2. **No contact lenses in the lab.** Contact lenses should not be worn during any investigations in which you are using chemicals (even if you are wearing goggles). In the event of an accident, chemicals can get behind contact lenses and cause serious damage before the lenses can be removed. If your doctor requires that you wear contact lenses instead of glasses, you should wear eye-cup safety goggles in the lab. Ask your doctor or your teacher how to use this very important and special eye protection.
3. **Personal apparel should be appropriate for laboratory work.** On lab days, avoid wearing long necklaces, dangling bracelets, bulky jewelry, and bulky or loose-fitting clothing. Long hair should be tied back. Loose, flopping, or dangling items may get caught in moving parts, accidentally contact electrical connections, or interfere with the investigation in some potentially hazardous manner. In addition, chemical fumes may react with some jewelry, such as pearls, and ruin them. Cotton clothing is preferable to wool, nylon, or polyesters. Wear shoes that will protect your feet from chemical spills and falling objects— no open-toed shoes or sandals and no shoes with woven leather straps.
4. **NEVER work alone in the laboratory.** Work in the lab only while supervised by your teacher. Do not leave equipment unattended while it is in operation.
5. **Only books and notebooks needed for the activity should be in the lab.** Only the lab notebook and perhaps the textbook should be used. Keep other books, backpacks, purses, and similar items in your desk, locker, or designated storage area.
6. **Read the entire activity before entering the lab.** Your teacher will review any applicable safety precautions before you begin the lab activity. If you are not sure of something, ask your teacher about it.
7. Always heed safety symbols and cautions in the instructions for the experiments, in handouts, and on posters in the room, and always heed cautions given verbally by your teacher. They are provided for your safety.
8. Know the proper fire drill procedures and the locations of fire exits and emergency equipment. Make sure you know the procedures to follow in case of a fire or other emergency.
9. **If your clothing catches on fire, do not run;** WALK to the safety shower, stand under the showerhead, and turn the water on. Call to your teacher while you do this.
10. **Report all accidents to the teacher** IMMEDIATELY, no matter how minor. In addition, if you get a headache or feel ill or dizzy, tell your teacher immediately.

11. **Report all spills to your teacher immediately.** Call your teacher, rather than cleaning a spill yourself. Your teacher will tell you if it is safe for you to clean up the spill. If it is not safe for you to clean up the spill, your teacher will know how the spill should be cleaned up safely.
12. If a lab directs you to design your own experiments, procedures must be approved by your teacher BEFORE you begin work.
13. DO NOT perform unauthorized experiments or use equipment or apparatus in a manner for which they were not intended. Use only materials and equipment listed in the activity equipment list or authorized by your teacher. Steps in a procedure should only be performed as described in the lab manual or as approved by your teacher.
14. **Stay alert while in the lab, and proceed with caution.** Be aware of others near you or your equipment when you are proceeding with the experiment. If you are not sure of how to proceed, ask your teacher for help.
15. **Horseplay in the lab is very dangerous.** Laboratory equipment and apparatus are not toys; never play in the lab or use lab time or equipment for anything other than their intended purpose.
16. Food, beverages, and chewing gum are NEVER permitted in the laboratory.
17. **NEVER taste chemicals.** Do not touch chemicals or allow them to contact areas of bare skin.
18. **Use extreme CAUTION when working with hot plates or other heating devices.** Keep your head, hands, hair, and clothing away from the flame or heating area, and turn the devices off when they are not in use. Remember that metal surfaces connected to the heated area will become hot by conduction. Gas burners should be lit only with a spark lighter. Make sure all heating devices and gas valves are turned off before leaving the laboratory. Never leave a hot plate or other heating device unattended when it is in use. Remember that many metal, ceramic, and glass items do not always look hot when they are heated. Allow all items to cool before storing them.
19. **Exercise caution when working with electrical equipment.** Do not use electrical equipment that has frayed or twisted wires. Be sure your hands are dry before you use electrical equipment. Do not let electrical cords dangle from work stations; dangling cords can cause tripping or electrical shocks.
20. **Keep work areas and apparatus clean and neat.** Always clean up any clutter made during the course of lab work, rearrange apparatus in an orderly manner, and report any damaged or missing items.
21. Always thoroughly wash your hands with soap and water at the conclusion of each investigation.

Name ______________________ Class ______________ Date ______________

Safety in the Field

Activities conducted outdoors require some advance planning to ensure a safe environment. The following general guidelines should be followed for fieldwork.

1. Know your mission. Your teacher will tell you the goal of the field trip in advance. Be sure to have your permission slip approved before the trip, and check to be sure that you have all necessary supplies for the day's activity.
2. Find out about on-site hazards before setting out. Determine whether poisonous plants or dangerous animals are likely to be present where you are going. Know how to identify these hazards. Find out about other hazards, such as steep or slippery terrain.
3. Wear protective clothing. Dress in a manner that will keep you warm, comfortable, and dry. Decide in advance whether you will need sunglasses, a hat, gloves, boots, or rain gear to suit the terrain and local weather conditions.
4. Do not approach or touch wild animals. If you see a threatening animal, call your teacher immediately. Avoid any living thing that may sting, bite, scratch, or otherwise cause injury.
5. Do not touch wild plants or pick wildflowers unless specifically instructed to do so by your teacher. Many wild plants can be irritating or toxic. Never taste any wild plant.
6. Do not wander away from others. Travel with a partner at all times. Stay within an area where you can be seen or heard in case you run into trouble.
7. Report all hazards or accidents to your teacher immediately. Even if the incident seems unimportant, let your teacher know what happened.
8. Maintain the safety of the environment. Do not remove anything from the field site without your teacher's permission. Stay on trails, when possible, to avoid trampling delicate vegetation. Never leave garbage behind at a field site. Leave natural areas as you found them.

Name ______________________ Class ______________ Date ______________

Laboratory Techniques

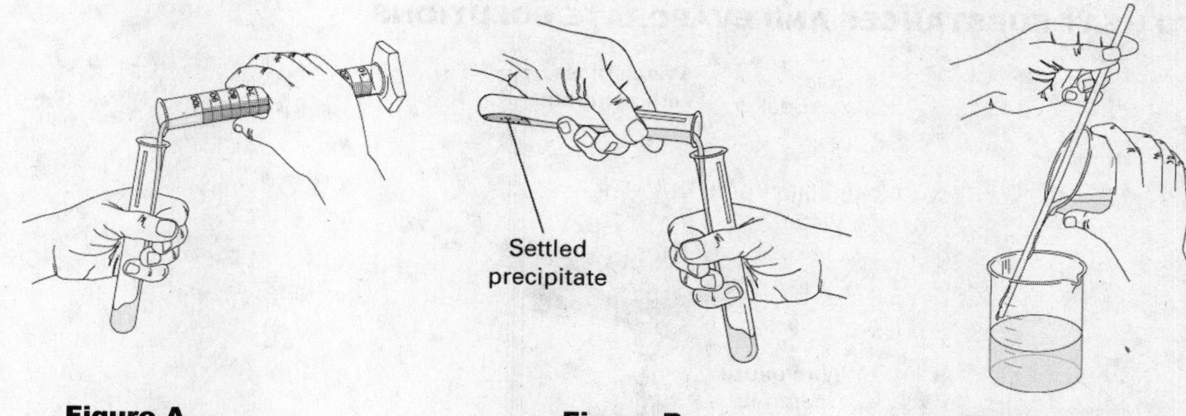

Figure A **Figure B** **Figure C**

HOW TO DECANT AND TRANSFER LIQUIDS

1. The safest way to transfer a liquid from a graduated cylinder to a test tube is shown in **Figure A**. The liquid is transferred at arm's length, with the elbows slightly bent. This position enables you to see what you are doing while maintaining steady control of the equipment.
2. Sometimes, liquids contain particles of insoluble solids that sink to the bottom of a test tube or beaker. Use one of the methods shown above to separate a supernatant (the clear fluid) from insoluble solids.

   a. **Figure B** shows the proper method of decanting a supernatant liquid from a test tube.

   b. **Figure C** shows the proper method of decanting a supernatant liquid from a beaker by using a stirring rod. The rod should touch the wall of the receiving container. Hold the stirring rod against the lip of the beaker containing the supernatant. As you pour, the liquid will run down the rod and fall into the beaker resting below. When you use this method, the liquid will not run down the side of the beaker from which you are pouring.

HOW TO HEAT SUBSTANCES AND EVAPORATE SOLUTIONS

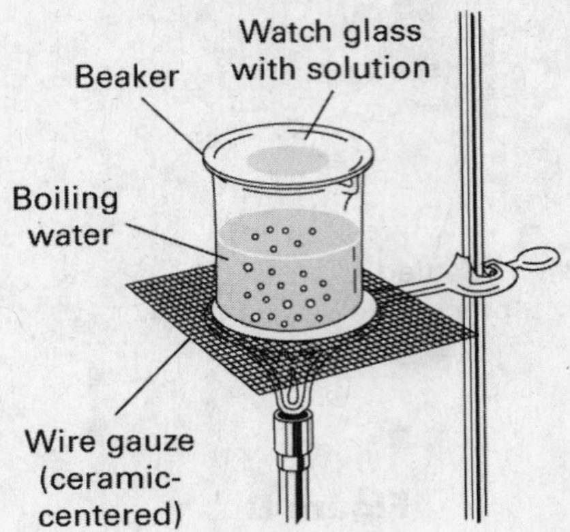

FIGURE D

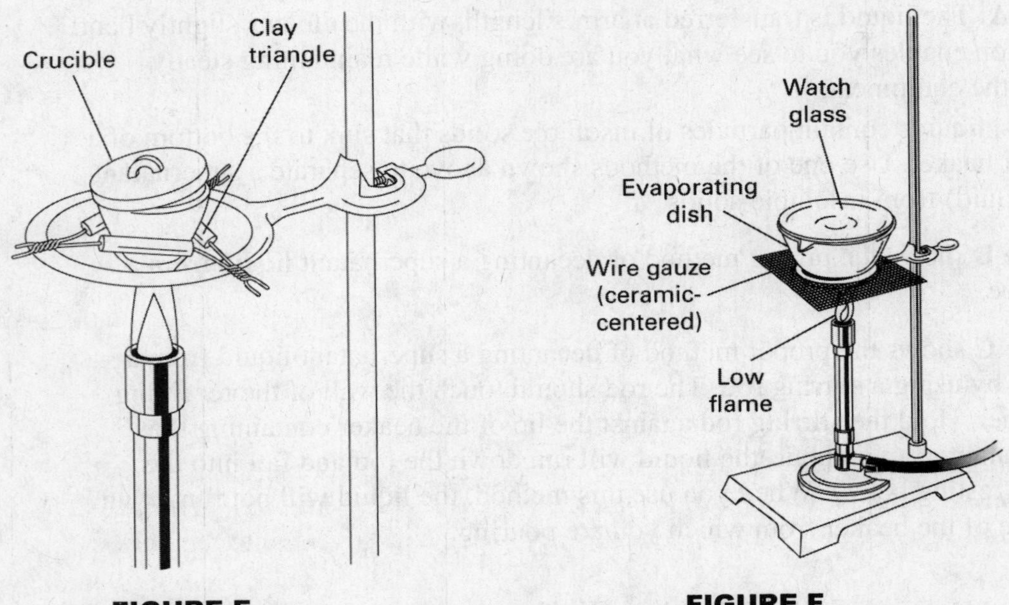

FIGURE E **FIGURE F**

1. Use care in selecting glassware for high-temperature heating. The glassware should be heat resistant.
2. When heating glassware by using a gas flame, use a ceramic-centered wire gauze to protect glassware from direct contact with the flame. Wire gauzes can withstand extremely high temperatures and will help prevent glassware from breaking. **Figure D** shows the proper setup for evaporating a solution over a water bath.
3. In some experiments, you are required to heat a substance to high temperatures in a porcelain crucible. Figure E shows the proper apparatus setup used to accomplish this task.
4. **Figure F** shows the proper setup for evaporating a solution in a porcelain evaporating dish with a watch glass cover that prevents spattering.

5. Glassware, porcelain, and iron rings that have been heated may look cool after they are removed from a heat source, but these items can still burn your skin even after several minutes of cooling. Use tongs, test-tube holders, or heat-resistant mitts and pads whenever you handle these pieces of apparatus.
6. You can test the temperature of beakers, ring stands, wire gauzes, or other pieces of apparatus that have been heated by holding the back of your hand close to their surfaces before grasping them. You will be able to feel any energy as heat generated from the hot surfaces. DO NOT TOUCH THE APPARATUS. Allow plenty of time for the apparatus to cool before handling.

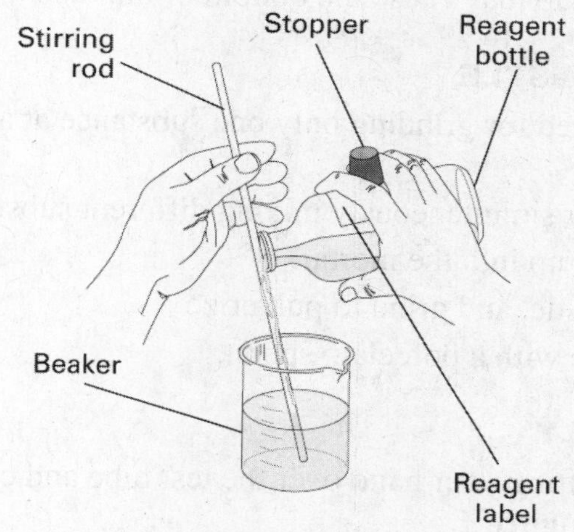

FIGURE G

HOW TO POUR LIQUID FROM A REAGENT BOTTLE

1. Read the label at least three times before using the contents of a reagent bottle.
2. Never lay the stopper of a reagent bottle on the lab table.
3. When pouring a caustic or corrosive liquid into a beaker, use a stirring rod to avoid drips and spills. Hold the stirring rod against the lip of the reagent bottle. Estimate the amount of liquid you need, and pour this amount along the rod, into the beaker. See **Figure G**.
4. Extra precaution should be taken when handling a bottle of acid. Remember the following important rules: Never add water to any concentrated acid, particularly sulfuric acid, because the mixture can splash and will generate a lot of energy as heat. To dilute any acid, add the acid to water in small quantities while stirring slowly. Remember the "triple A's"—*Always Add Acid* to water.
5. Examine the outside of the reagent bottle for any liquid that has dripped down the bottle or spilled on the counter top. Your teacher will show you the proper procedures for cleaning up a chemical spill.
6. Never pour reagents back into stock bottles. At the end of the experiment, your teacher will tell you how to dispose of any excess chemicals.

Laboratory Techniques continued

HOW TO HEAT MATERIAL IN A TEST TUBE

1. Check to see that the test tube is heat resistant.
2. Always use a test tube holder or clamp when heating a test tube.
3. Never point a heated test tube at anyone, because the liquid may splash out of the test tube.
4. Never look down into the test tube while heating it.
5. Heat the test tube from the upper portions of the tube downward, and continuously move the test tube, as shown in **Figure H**. Do not heat any one spot on the test tube. Otherwise, a pressure buildup may cause the bottom of the tube to blow out.

HOW TO USE A MORTAR AND PESTLE

1. A mortar and pestle should be used for grinding only one substance at a time. See **Figure I**.
2. Never use a mortar and pestle for simultaneously mixing different substances.
3. Place the substance to be broken up into the mortar.
4. Pound the substance with the pestle, and grind to pulverize.
5. Remove the powdered substance with a porcelain spoon.

HOW TO DETECT ODORS SAFELY

1. Test for the odor of gases by wafting your hand over the test tube and cautiously sniffing the fumes as shown in **Figure J**.
2. Do not inhale any fumes directly.
3. Use a fume hood whenever poisonous or irritating fumes are present. DO NOT waft and sniff poisonous or irritating fumes.

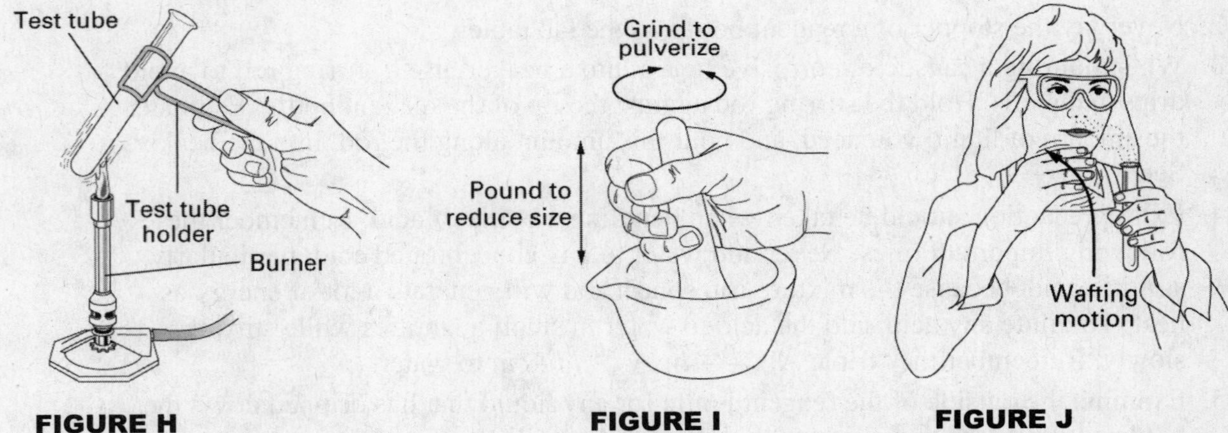

FIGURE H **FIGURE I** **FIGURE J**

Name ______________________ Class ______________ Date ______________

Student Safety Quiz

Circle the letter of the BEST answer.

1. Before starting an investigation or lab procedure, you should
   a. try an experiment of your own
   b. open all containers and packages
   c. read all directions and make sure you understand them
   d. handle all the equipment to become familiar with it
2. When pouring chemicals between containers, you should hold the containers over
   a. the floor or a waste basket
   b. a fire blanket or an oven mitt
   c. an eyewash station or a water fountain
   d. a sink or your work area
3. If you get hurt or injured in any way, you should
   a. tell your teacher immediately
   b. find bandages or a first aid kit
   c. go to the principal's office
   d. get help after you finish the lab
4. If your glassware is chipped or broken, you should
   a. use it only for solid materials
   b. give it to your teacher
   c. put it back into the storage cabinet
   d. increase the damage so that it is obvious
5. If you have unused chemicals after finishing a procedure, you should
   a. pour them down a sink or drain
   b. mix them all together in a bucket
   c. put them back into their original containers
   d. throw them away where your teacher tells you to

6. If electrical equipment has a frayed cord, you should
   a. unplug the equipment by pulling on the cord
   b. let the cord hang over the side of a counter or table
   c. tell your teacher about the problem immediately
   d. wrap tape around the cord to repair it

7. If you need to determine the odor of a chemical or a solution, you should
   a. use your hand to bring fumes from the container to your nose
   b. bring the container under your nose and inhale deeply
   c. tell your teacher immediately
   d. use odor-sensing equipment

8. When working with materials that might fly into the air and hurt someone's eye, you should wear
   a. goggles
   b. an apron
   c. gloves
   d. a hat

9. Before doing experiments involving a heat source, you should know the location of the
   a. door
   b. windows
   c. fire extinguisher
   d. overhead lights

10. If you get a chemical in your eye, you should
    a. wash your hands immediately
    b. put the lid back on the chemical container
    c. wait to see if your eye becomes irritated
    d. use the eyewash right away

11. When working with a flame or heat source, you should
    a. tie back long hair or hair that hangs in front of your eyes
    b. heat substances or objects inside a closed container
    c. touch an object with your bare hand to see how hot it is
    d. throw hot objects into the trash when you are done with them

12. As you cut with a knife or other sharp instrument, you should move the instrument
    a. toward you
    b. away from you
    c. vertically
    d. horizontally

Name ______________________ Class ______________ Date ______________

LAB SAFETY QUIZ

Answer Key

1. C	5. D	9. C
2. D	6. C	10. D
3. A	7. A	11. A
4. B	8. A	12. B

Name ______________________________ Class ________________ Date ________________

Student Safety Contract

Read carefully the Student Safety Contract below. Then, fill in your name in the first blank, date the contract, and sign it.

Student Safety Contract

I will

- read the lab investigation before coming to class
- wear personal protective equipment as directed to protect my eyes, face, hands, and body while conducting class activities
- follow all instructions given by the teacher
- conduct myself in a responsible manner at all times in a laboratory situation

I, ______________________________, have read and agree to abide by the safety regulations as set forth above and any additional printed instructions provided by my teacher or the school district.

I agree to follow all other written and oral instructions given in class.

Signature: ______________________________

Date: ______________________________

QUICK LAB GUIDED *Inquiry*

What's in the Box? GENERAL

Small groups
25 minutes

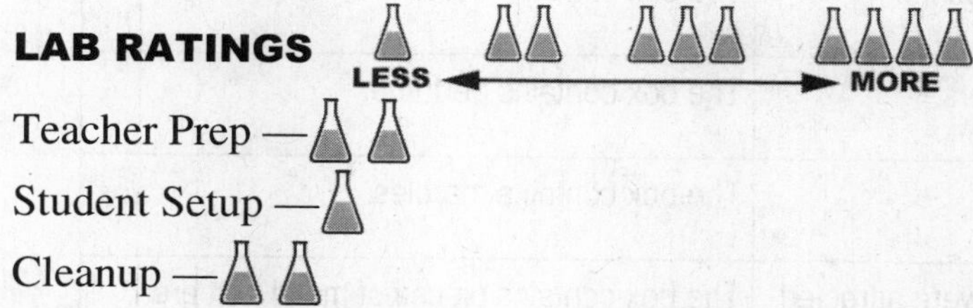

MATERIALS

For whole class
- assortment of mystery objects (magnets, sand, small inflated balloons, alarm clock, marbles, small bells, cotton balls, air freshener, pencils, etc.)
- assortment of tools for investigation (magnets, balance)
- marker
- packing tape
- shoeboxes with lids (one for each group)

For each student
- safety goggles

SAFETY INFORMATION

Remind students to review all safety cautions and icons before beginning this lab. Have students wear safety goggles if you are using marbles, sand, or any other particulate.

TEACHER NOTES

Place several mystery objects in each box, so that students must make inferences from a variety of observations. Seal each box closed with the packing tape, and label each box with the marker. This activity works best if the mystery objects engage a variety of senses such as sound, smell, and touch. To have students investigate the sense of touch, cut a hole in the lid of the box and attach a glove or sock to the opening so that students can touch the contents of the box without directly observing them. To investigate the sense of smell, perforate the lid of the box and place objects such as flowers or a small bag of chopped onions in the box. Place the boxes at different stations throughout the classroom, and make sure that groups visit each station.

Skills Focus Making Observations, Making Predictions

My Notes

MODIFICATION FOR DIRECTED *Inquiry*

Demonstrate for students the process of identifying the characteristics of the object(s) in a box. Walk them through tests they can carry out, questions they can ask, and observations they can make.

MODIFICATION FOR INDEPENDENT *Inquiry*

Have each student group prepare the mystery boxes themselves and exchange them with other student groups. To focus specifically on modeling and mapping skills, have student teams create a "maze" inside their box using pieces of cardboard and tape or glue. Teams should place a marble inside each box and seal the box. Then, teams can exchange boxes and challenge each other to create a detailed map of the box's interior based on movement of the marble when the box is tilted.

Quick Lab continued

Answer Key

2. Sample answer:

Box Number	Observations	Prediction
1	The contents made a ringing sound.	The box contains bells.
2	The contents smelled like flowers.	The box contains perfume.
3	The contents rolled around.	The box contains marbles.
4	The contents were heavy and were attracted to magnets.	The box contains pieces of metal that are attracted to magnets.

4. Sample answer: Two of our predictions were accurate, and three of our predictions were wrong. It was easy to accurately predict the contents of the boxes when only one object was in the box. However, it was harder to accurately predict the contents when more than one object was in the box.

5. Scientists investigate many things that cannot be directly observed. For example, scientists investigate the structure of Earth, the movement of earthquake waves, and events that happened in Earth's early history. In addition to using their senses to gather data, scientists use technology such as remote sensing. Then, they make inferences based on their observations and use models to investigate objects and processes that cannot be directly observed.

6. Scientific models help scientists investigate objects and processes that cannot be directly observed. Models can help scientists understand complex processes and predict the effects of changing variables. Models are also limited by the fact that they are representations of objects or processes, so they can distort or misrepresent the object or process a scientist is investigating.

Name ______________________ Class ______________ Date ______________

QUICK LAB GUIDED Inquiry

What's in the Box?

In this lab, you will explore how scientists investigate phenomena that they cannot directly observe.

OBJECTIVES

- Describe how scientists gather data from indirect observation.
- Explain the benefits and limitations of scientific models.

MATERIALS

For each group
- sealed boxes containing mystery objects

For each student
- safety goggles

PROCEDURE

1. The sealed **boxes** in your classroom each contain mystery objects. Your group will investigate each of the boxes and attempt to identify the contents of the boxes without opening them.
2. As a group, investigate each of the boxes. Record your observations and predictions in the table below.

Box Number	Observations	Prediction
1		
2		
3		
4		

3. Compare your group's predictions with the predictions made by other groups. Discuss each group's observations and predictions.

Quick Lab continued

4 Your teacher will open each box. Compare your predictions with the contents of the box. Were your predictions accurate? Why or why not?

5 How was this activity similar to the ways that scientists investigate objects or processes that they cannot directly observe?

6 What are the benefits and limitations of using models to investigate objects or processes that cannot be directly observed?

QUICK LAB INDEPENDENT Inquiry

Investigating the Unseen GENERAL

Student pairs
30 minutes

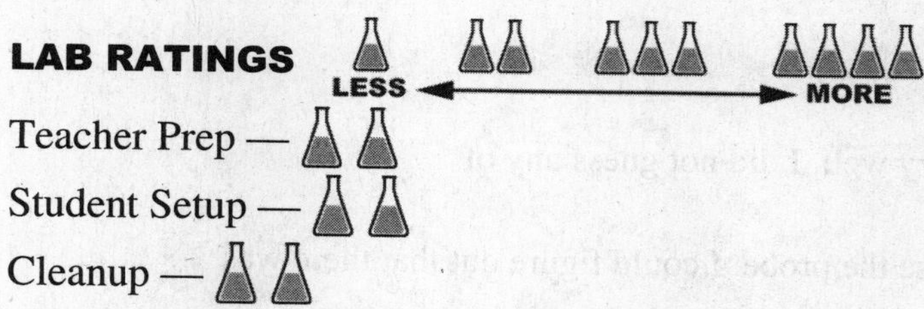

MATERIALS

For each pair
- modeling clay
- paper clips (2)
- toothpicks (2)
- various small objects, such as steel ball bearings, short screws, hex nuts, staples

SAFETY INFORMATION

Remind students to review all safety cautions and icons before beginning this lab. This lab involves manipulation of hard objects, which may pose a piercing hazard.

My Notes

TEACHER NOTES

In this activity, students identify the interior components of an object. Each student prepares a golf ball-sized clay ball with up to three small metal objects inside. They do this without letting their partner see the objects being placed in the clay. Partners exchange clay samples. Each student makes and records their guesses as to what object(s) are present in the sample.

Students then decide on a method to assess the nature of the object(s) using a toothpick or a paper clip and carry out their method. Students record the characteristics of the objects such as number of objects, size, smoothness, and shape. Based on these characteristics, each student draws a conclusion about the identities of the objects in their sample. Students then break apart the clay to reveal the objects and compare the actual identities with inferred identities determined from the probing procedure. Students will also analyze whether one type of probe (toothpick or paper clip) was more effective than the other for obtaining information.

Tip This activity will help students understand that scientific explanations are based on empirical evidence, not on feelings or unguided guessing.

Skills Focus Making Observations, Drawing Conclusions, Comparing Methods

MODIFICATION FOR GUIDED Inquiry

For the Guided Inquiry option, instruct students to use the toothpick or paper clip as a probe.

Quick Lab continued

Answer Key

3. Accept all reasonable answers.
4. Accept all reasonable answers. Sample answer: I will poke the toothpick into the clay several times to see where the object is and to get an idea of its size and shape.
5. Accept all reasonable answers.
6. Accept all reasonable answers.
7. Accept all reasonable answers.
8. Sample answer: Guessing did not work very well. I did not guess any of the objects correctly.
9. Sample answer: It was more effective to use the probe. I could figure out that there was a screw inside my sample.
10. Sample answer: Most students did better at using the probe than guessing. The paper clip was better because it didn't break while pushing into the clay.

Name ______________________ Class ______________ Date ______________

QUICK LAB INDEPENDENT Inquiry

Investigating the Unseen

In this lab, you will develop a method for gathering data about a system that you cannot see.

OBJECTIVES

- Use empirical evidence to draw conclusions about objects that cannot be seen.

MATERIALS

For each pair

- modeling clay
- paper clips (2)
- toothpicks (2)
- various small objects, such as steel ball bearings, short screws, hex nuts, staples

PROCEDURE

1. Take an amount of modeling clay roughly equal to the size of a golf ball. Select one, two, or three different metal objects to place inside the clay. Work the clay around the objects until they are completely hidden from view. As you do this, do not let your partner see which objects you are using.
2. Trade clay samples with your partner.
3. Using visual observations alone, guess the object(s) hidden inside your piece of clay.

 ____

 ____

 ____

4. Think of a way to use the paper clip or the toothpick to gather more information about the object(s) inside the clay without using them to break apart the clay. The idea is to figure out a way to gather information about the objects inside without looking at the objects. Write your plan below.

 ____

 ____

 ____

5. Carry out your plan from Step 4. What additional information about the objects are you able to gather using your method?

 ____

 ____

 ____

 ____

 ____

 ____

Quick Lab continued

6 Based on your observations from Step 5, write down the identities of the objects you think are in the clay.

____

____

____

7 Break apart the clay and note the actual objects inside.

____

____

____

8 Compare your original guesses with the identities of the objects revealed in Step 7. How well did it work to guess the objects hidden in the clay?

____

____

____

9 Compare your conclusions from Step 6 with the identities of the objects revealed in Step 7. How well did it work to probe the contents of the clay to determine their identities? Which approach was more effective, guessing or using a probe to gather information about the objects? Explain.

____

____

____

____

____

10 Compare your results with those of others in the class. Did anyone do better at guessing than at using a probe? Was there a difference between using the paper clip versus the toothpick?

____

____

____

____

QUICK LAB GUIDED *Inquiry*

Design Procedures GENERAL

Individual student

20 minutes for initial setup, 5 minutes a day for a week

MATERIALS

For each student

- green plant
- other materials to carry out your experiment
- reference materials

My Notes

LAB RATINGS

LESS ⟷ MORE

Teacher Prep — 1

Student Setup — 2

Cleanup — 1

SAFETY INFORMATION

Remind students to review all lab safety icons before beginning the lab. Tell students that plants are living things, and so special care needs to be taken to ensure their safety. As always, because they are handling lab materials, instruct students to wash their hands thoroughly.

TEACHER NOTES

In this activity, students will design an experiment to show how plants respond to their environment. Begin by discussing how all living things respond to their environments and ask students what are some things that plants need. Give some information about plant tropisms and have students design their experiments to see tropisms in action.

Although this is a guided inquiry, help students through the design process using the Teaching prompts. Encourage students to use the Design Process worksheet as they brainstorm.

Tip This activity gives students an understanding of how scientists need to think logically, but also creatively.

Skills Focus Forming Hypotheses, Developing Procedures, Evaluating Procedures

MODIFICATION FOR DIRECTED *Inquiry*

Give students a question to answer: "How do plants respond to light?" Guide students as they research the topic and form their hypothesis. Then work together as a large group to design an experiment and carry it out. When it is done, discuss how the design process worked.

Quick Lab continued

Answer Key

1. Answers will vary.
   Teacher Prompt If necessary, provide students with suggestions for how plants respond to light, gravity, and in some cases, touch.
2. Answers will vary.
   Teacher Prompt Research is an important part of the process. Have students list reasons why research is important in the design process.
3. Answers will vary.
   Teacher Prompt Provide guidance to students who cannot readily think of a design. Refer students to the Design Process worksheet for more support designing a scientific process.
4. Answers will vary.
   Teacher Prompt Make sure you have the materials students will need for their experiments ready.
5. Accept all reasonable sketches.
6. Answers will vary.
   Teacher Prompt Ask why it is important to be able to repeat the process and arrive at the same result. Guide students who need help to redesign their experiments.
7. Answers will vary.
   Teacher Prompt Approve all activities for safety concerns. Even if you know an experiment may not prove the hypothesis proposed, allow students to carry out the procedure anyway.
8. Answers will vary.
   Teacher Prompt Tell students that even if they do not get the results they were expecting, the experiment was not a failure. Part of the scientific process is trial and error.
9. Sample answer: I thought creatively to come up with a question, a hypothesis, and a design setup.
10. Sample answer: I thought logically by following the design process and by doing research before developing my hypothesis.

Name ______________________ Class ______________ Date ______________

QUICK LAB GUIDED *Inquiry*

Designing a Procedure

When scientists begin an experiment, they need to think creatively to identify a problem and a setup that they can use to test their hypothesis. But they also need to think logically and follow set steps. In this lab, you will think both creatively and logically as you try to design a procedure that shows how plants respond to stimuli.

OBJECTIVES

- Use creativity while designing a procedure.
- Follow the scientific process for carrying out experiments.

MATERIALS

For each student

- green plant
- other materials to carry out your experiment
- reference materials

PROCEDURE

1. Ask yourself a question about plants and how they respond to things in the environment. Think creatively.

   ____
   ____
   ____

2. Think creatively to write a hypothesis to answer your question. Do research if needed.

   ____
   ____
   ____

3. How can you test your hypothesis? Think creatively to design an experiment.

   ____
   ____
   ____
   ____
   ____
   ____
   ____
   ____

Name ______________________ Class ______________ Date ______________

Quick Lab continued

4. Gather the materials you will need. List them here.

____

____

____

____

5. Set up your prototype. Draw a sketch of it here.

6. Evaluate your plan. Could it be repeated and get the same results? If not, redesign your plan.

____

____

____

____

____

____

____

Name ______________________ Class ______________ Date ______________

Quick Lab continued

7. Have your teacher review your plan before you carry it out. Record your observations here.

8. Reevaluate your hypothesis. Did you get the outcome you were expecting? Explain.

9. How did you think creatively during this experiment?

10. How did you think logically during this experiment?

QUICK LAB DIRECTED Inquiry

The Importance of Replication GENERAL

Small groups
30 minutes

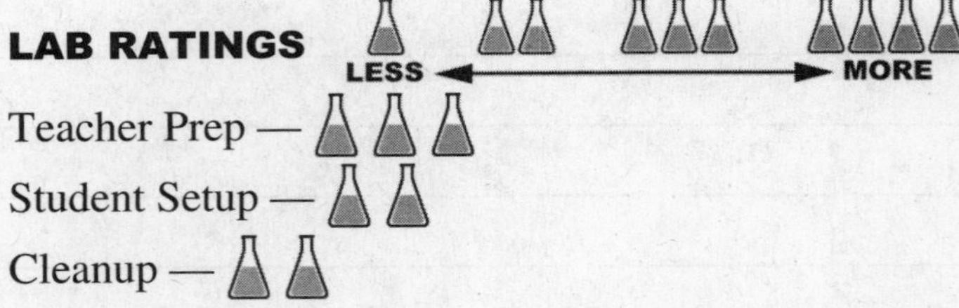

MATERIALS

For each group
- balance
- ball bearing, metal
- graduated cylinder
- modeling clay formed into different shapes (one set for the whole class)
- paper, graph (1 sheet)
- ruler, metric

For each student
- gloves
- lab apron
- safety goggles

SAFETY INFORMATION

Remind students to review all safety cautions and icons before beginning this lab. Water on the floor can be a slipping hazard. Make sure all spills are wiped up immediately. Modeling clay can stain hands and clothing. Students should wear gloves and lab aprons while handling modeling clay.

TEACHER NOTES

In this activity, students determine the densities of differently shaped objects made of the same material. You should form the modeling clay into a variety of different shapes, such as a cube, a sphere, and a cylinder. There should be the same number of shapes as there are student groups. Make one set of shapes for the whole class; each group will measure the mass and volume of each shape. The mass of each shape does not matter. You should modify one of the shapes by placing a metal ball bearing inside it (the ball bearing should not be visible to the students) so that its density is significantly higher than that of the other shapes. Students should compare their results for each shape and use the replication of measurements to help them identify the outlier.
If you wish, you may explain how the slope of a line on a mass vs. volume plot is related to the density of the objects.

Tip This activity may help students better understand the importance of replication of results in determining whether results are valid.

Skills Focus Organizing Data, Constructing Graphs, Comparing Results

My Notes

MODIFICATION FOR GUIDED Inquiry

Have students work as a class to develop a method for testing the reliability of each group's measurements and comparing the data. When the class has come up with an appropriate procedure, have them carry it out. Students should share their data with the class.

Quick Lab continued

MODIFICATION FOR INDEPENDENT *Inquiry*

Have students devise a method for confirming the accuracy of the measuring apparatus available in your classroom. Students should explain how their method will allow them to confirm the accuracy of each tool. Allow students to carry out all reasonable procedures. They should share their results with the class. If you wish, have students post their results on the wall of the classroom so that other students using the same equipment can have access to the results.

Answer Key

2. Answers will vary.
3. Answers will vary, but all the data points except one (the shape you have weighted with the ball bearing) should lie approximately along a straight line.
4. Sample answer: No, not all the objects have the same density. The sphere seems to be much denser than all the other shapes. Except for the sphere, all the shapes have the same density.
5. Sample answer: Our balance or graduated cylinder might not be accurate, or we might not have used it correctly. We might have recorded our data points incorrectly.
6. Sample answer: Our group's results were very similar to all the other groups' results. All the shapes except for the sphere have the same density. The sphere is much denser than the other shapes.
7. Sample answer: Knowing that all the groups found that the sphere was denser than the other objects makes us more confident that the sphere is actually denser and that we did not just make a mistake in our measurements.

Name ______________________ Class ______________ Date ________________

QUICK LAB DIRECTED Inquiry

The Importance of Replication

In this lab, you will determine the densities of several objects made of the same material. You will compare your results to those of others in the class.

OBJECTIVE

- Explain why scientific investigations should be replicable.

MATERIALS

For each group
- balance
- graduated cylinder
- modeling clay, different shapes
- paper, graph (1 sheet)
- ruler, metric

For each student
- gloves
- lab apron
- safety goggles

PROCEDURE

1. In the space below, create a data table to record the mass and volume of each **clay shape**.

2. Measure the mass and volume of each clay shape using the measuring apparatus provided. Record the results in your data table.

3. On a piece of **graph paper**, make a scatter plot of the masses and volumes of the different shapes. Plot mass on the vertical axis and volume on the horizontal axis.

4. If your objects all have the same density, they should form a straight line on your graph. Based on your data, do all the objects have the same density? Explain your answer.

____

____

____

____

____

____

Quick Lab continued

5. What are some possible sources of error in your data?

6. Compare your results to those of other groups. What can you conclude about the densities of the different shapes?

7. How does having multiple sets of measurements for each shape help you evaluate your data?

FIELD LAB GUIDED Inquiry **AND** INDEPENDENT Inquiry

Investigating Soil Microorganisms GENERAL

Student pairs

One 45-minute class period and about 5 minutes/day for 10 days

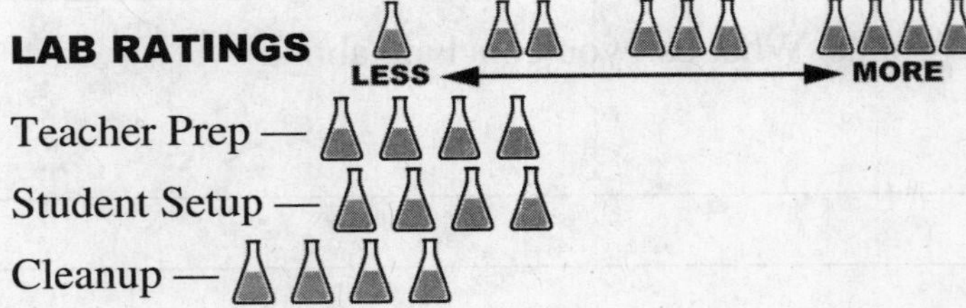

SAFETY INFORMATION

Remind students to review all safety cautions and icons before beginning this lab. Remind students to avoid contamination of their samples and of their workspaces and bodies. Students should not open the petri dishes once they have been sealed. Make sure students wash their hands with soap and water after each lab session.

Although most of the bacteria cultured in a lab such as this one do not present a general risk to health or safety, it is important to teach students the proper methods for working with microorganisms in a lab and for disposing of materials that may be contaminated with bacteria. Do not dispose of any of this lab's materials in the general classroom waste bins. Prepare specific bins for the disposal of used swabs, gloves, petri dishes, and other contaminated items. Follow your school and/or district guidelines for disposal of potentially hazardous wastes. Sterilize all lab surfaces with a diluted bleach solution at the end of each lab session.

MATERIALS

For each pair

- magnifying lens
- marker, permanent
- petri dishes containing sterile nutrient agar (4)
- plastic bags (3)
- ruler, metric
- spoon
- swab, cotton (4)
- tape, transparent or masking
- water, distilled

For each student

- gloves
- lab apron
- safety goggles

My Notes

____

____

____

____

____

TEACHER NOTES

In this activity, students take soil from various locations and use it to characterize differences in microorganism types living at the sampled locations. Each soil sample is mixed with distilled water, and a small amount of the mixture is spread on an agar plate with a cotton swab. As a control, distilled water (without any soil) is spread on an agar plate in the same manner. Students observe the agar plates over a period of two weeks, recording their observations in a notebook. A digital camera can be used to take photos that include the ruler as a scale. If a camera is not available, drawings and written descriptions can be recorded instead. Students describe the differences in microorganism colonies produced on the various plates and use graphs to summarize the number and sizes of the colonies observed. Point out to students that "growing a culture" means allowing one or more small microorganisms to multiply until there is a large enough number of individual microorganisms to be seen and *not* that a single microorganism grows until it is large enough to be seen.

Field Lab continued

Pre-poured agar plates can be purchased from a biological supply house. To minimize the risk of contamination from airborne bacteria, have students lift the petri dish lids only slightly when treating the agar. An alternative to prepared, sterile agar plates is to prepare liquid nutrient agar that is sterilized and poured into dishes. This should be done shortly before the time of use (same day), to minimize bacterial growth before beginning the lab. Potato slices can also be used instead of agar plates. Keep the swabbed potato slices in labeled, airtight plastic bags. If an incubator is available, the plates can be incubated at 37° C to speed up the fungal/bacterial growth.

Tip Explain that students will observe fungal colonies on their plates as well as bacterial colonies. Tell them that bacterial colonies tend to have shiny surfaces, while fungal colonies usually do not. Download materials students can use to identify colonies that develop.

Student Tip Treat all bacteria as if they are pathogens. Follow all of your teacher's safety procedures. Never reopen a petri dish that has been inoculated with bacteria. Dispose of all contaminated materials in the appropriate waste disposal container, and wash your hands after handling the materials.

Skills Focus Practicing Lab Techniques, Drawing Conclusions

MODIFICATION FOR DIRECTED Inquiry

For the Directed Inquiry option, explain how students should include a control agar plate as part of the experiment.

Answer Key for GUIDED Inquiry

DEVELOP A PLAN

4. Accept all reasonable answers.
5. Sample answer: We will dip a cotton swab into distilled water and use that to swipe an agar plate as a way to make a control plate.

ANALYZE RESULTS

9. Accept all reasonable answers.
   Teacher prompt What kinds of features can you see and measure?
10. Accept all reasonable answers.
    Teacher prompt How could you include data from the different agar plates on the graph?

Field Lab continued

DRAW CONCLUSIONS

11. Accept all reasonable answers.

Connect TO THE ESSENTIAL QUESTION

12. Sample answer: The control allows us to know what microorganisms are present in the water, the agar, or the cotton swab that have nothing to do with the soil samples we were trying to analyze. We needed the control so that we could be sure which microorganisms came from the soil in our experimental plates.
Teacher prompt What information comes from the control plate?

Answer Key for INDEPENDENT Inquiry

DEVELOP A PLAN

4. Accept all reasonable answers.

5. Sample answer: We will dip a cotton swab into distilled water and use that to swipe an agar plate as a way to make a control plate.

6. Sample answer: We can use a digital camera to take photos as part of the record. We will measure the growth of individual colonies with the ruler. The ruler can be used as a scale in our photos.
Teacher prompt How do we typically create visual records?

ANALYZE RESULTS

9. Accept all reasonable answers.
Teacher prompt What kinds of features can you see and measure?

10. Accept all reasonable answers.
Teacher prompt How could you include data from the different agar plates on the graph?

DRAW CONCLUSIONS

11. Accept all reasonable answers.

Connect TO THE ESSENTIAL QUESTION

12. Sample answer: The control allows us to know what microorganisms are present in the water, the agar, or the cotton swab that have nothing to do with the soil samples we were trying to analyze. We needed the control so that we could be sure which microorganisms came from the soil in our experimental plates.
Teacher prompt What information comes from the control plate?

Name ______________________ Class ______________ Date ______________

FIELD LAB GUIDED *Inquiry*

Investigating Soil Microorganisms

In this lab, you will collect soil samples and test them for their microorganism content. Because microorganisms are so small and difficult to detect, you will need to grow cultures of these microbes over a period of time in order to observe them and to make comparisons between the various soil samples you collect.

OBJECTIVE

- Sample soil from various locations in order to characterize the different microorganisms present.

MATERIALS

For each pair
- magnifying lens
- marker, permanent
- petri dishes containing sterile nutrient agar (4)
- plastic bags (3)
- ruler, metric
- spoon
- swab, cotton (4)
- tape, transparent or masking
- water, distilled

For each student
- gloves
- lab apron
- safety goggles

PROCEDURE

ASK A QUESTION

1. Soil microorganisms are important in decomposing organic matter in terrestrial environments. In this lab, you will investigate the following question: Do soils differ in the types of microorganisms that can be found?

2. You can culture microorganisms from a location by using a cotton swab to swipe a surface and then touching the cotton swab to agar containing nutrients that allow microorganisms to grow.

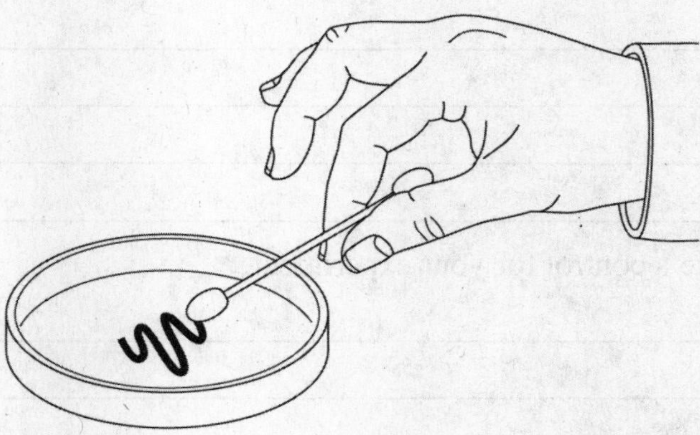

3. After swabbing the agar plates, seal them, label them, and store them upside down in a warm, dark environment so that the microorganisms can grow.

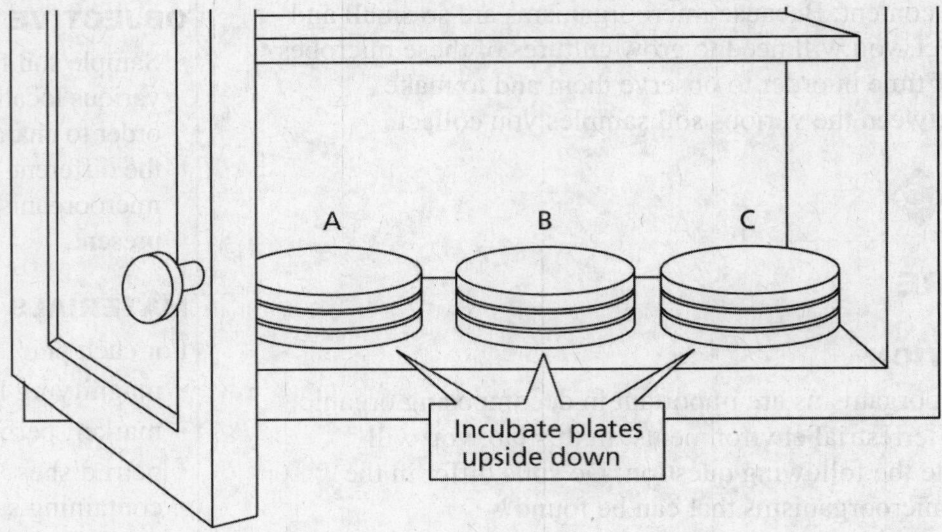

DEVELOP A PLAN

4. Work with your lab partner to develop a plan of study so that you can answer the question posed above. How can you use the materials provided to study differences in microorganisms in soil samples?

____

____

____

____

5. Explain how you plan to create a control for your experiment.

____

____

6. Obtain your teacher's approval for your plan.

MAKE OBSERVATIONS

7. Carry out your plan and make initial observations of your agar plates before you begin incubating them. Record your observations in a notebook. Use a digital camera to take photos as part of the record if possible. If a camera is not available, drawings and written descriptions will suffice.

Field Lab continued

8. Observe the agar plates every day over a period of two weeks to record the growth of microorganisms on the agar plates. Measure the growth of individual colonies with the ruler.

ANALYZE RESULTS

9. **Summarizing Results** Describe the differences in microorganisms between the soil samples.

____

____

____

10. **Graphing Data** Graph the number and size of the colonies over time.

DRAW CONCLUSIONS

11. **Comparing Samples** Was there any difference between the soil samples in the number, size, and type of soil microorganisms?

____

____

____

Connect TO THE ESSENTIAL QUESTION

12. **Evaluating Methods** What was the purpose of the control plate in your experiment? Why was this important to include?

____

____

____

Name ______________________ Class ______________ Date ______________

FIELD LAB INDEPENDENT *Inquiry*

Investigating Soil Microorganisms

In this lab, you will collect soil samples and test them for their microorganism content. Because microorganisms are so small and difficult to detect, you will need to grow cultures of these microbes over a period of time in order to observe them and to make comparisons between the various soil samples you collect.

OBJECTIVE

- Sample soil from various locations in order to characterize the different microorganisms present.

MATERIALS

For each pair

- magnifying lens
- marker, permanent
- petri dishes containing sterile nutrient agar (4)
- plastic bags (3)
- ruler, metric
- spoon
- swab, cotton (4)
- tape, transparent or masking
- water, distilled

For each student

- gloves
- lab apron
- safety goggles

PROCEDURE

ASK A QUESTION

1. Soil microorganisms are important in decomposing organic matter in terrestrial environments. In this lab, you will investigate the following question: Do soils differ in the types of microorganisms that can be found?

2. You can culture microorganisms from a location by using a cotton swab to swipe a surface and then touching the cotton swab to agar containing nutrients that allow microorganisms to grow.

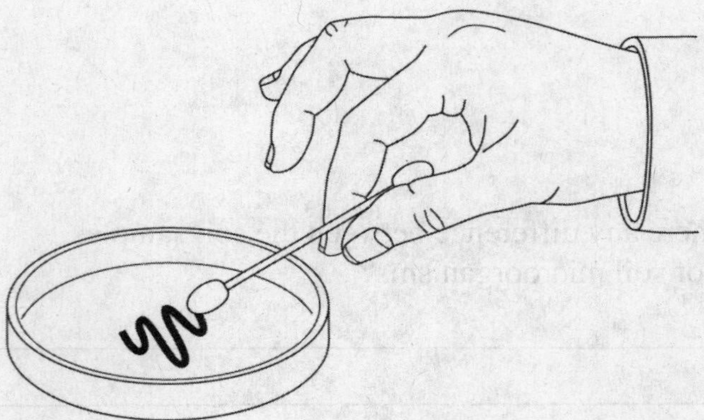

Field Lab continued

3. After swabbing the agar plates, seal them, label them, and store them upside down in a warm, dark environment so that the microorganisms can grow.

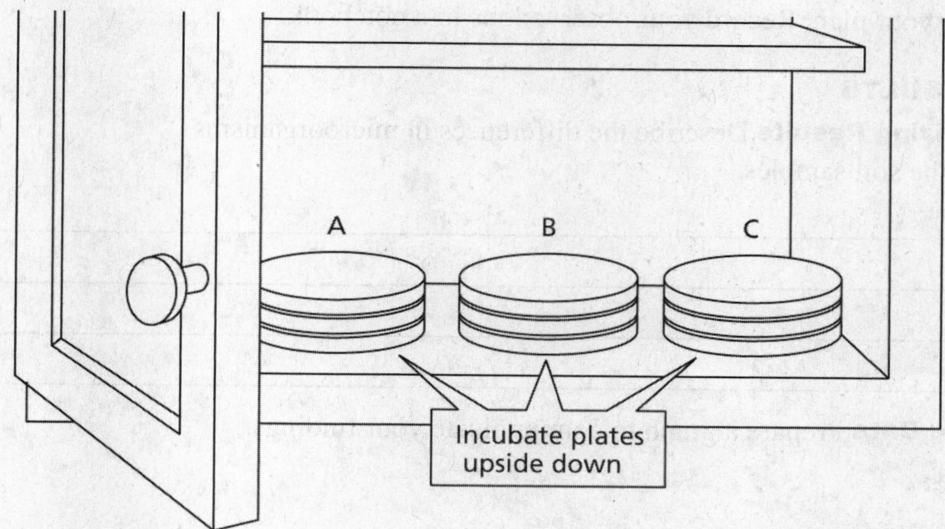

DEVELOP A PLAN

4. Work with your lab partner to develop a plan of study so that you can answer the question posed above. How can you use the materials provided to study differences in microorganisms in soil samples?

____

____

____

____

5. Explain how you plan to create a control for your experiment.

____

____

6. Explain how you plan to record observations and what quantitative measurements you plan to make using the ruler.

____

____

____

Name ______________________ Class ______________ Date ______________

Field Lab continued

7. Obtain your teacher's approval for your plan.

MAKE OBSERVATIONS

8. Carry out your plan. Record your observations in a notebook.

ANALYZE RESULTS

9. **Summarizing Results** Describe the differences in microorganisms between the soil samples.

____

____

____

____

10. **Graphing Data** Prepare a graph to communicate your findings.

Name ______________________ Class ______________ Date ______________

Field Lab continued

DRAW CONCLUSIONS

11 **Comparing Samples** Was there any difference between the soil samples in the number, size, and type of soil microorganisms?

____

____

____

____

Connect TO THE ESSENTIAL QUESTION

12 **Evaluating Methods** What was the purpose of the control plate in your experiment? Why was this important to include?

____

____

____

____

QUICK LAB GUIDED *Inquiry*

Pluto on Trial GENERAL

Small groups
20 minutes

MATERIALS

For each group
- chart paper
- markers
- research materials

LAB RATINGS

LESS ⟷ MORE

Teacher Prep — 1
Student Setup — 1
Cleanup — 1

My Notes

SAFETY INFORMATION

Remind students to review all safety cautions and icons before beginning this lab.

TEACHER NOTES

In this activity, students will investigate how scientific descriptions of the solar system have changed over time. Students will learn that scientists change scientific information after new evidence is gathered. To explore these ideas, students will conduct a classroom trial of Pluto's planetary status. Depending on the available time, you can decide whether to conduct this activity as a full "trial"(including a jury) or as a classroom debate or discussion. Encourage students to represent their ideas visually, using charts and illustrations to support their claims. Students may argue that Pluto is not a planet because it is not officially recognized as a planet. Consider making such claims "inadmissible" in your classroom courtroom by requiring that students support their claims with scientific evidence.

Skills Focus Conducting Research, Gathering Evidence, Evaluating Evidence

MODIFICATION FOR INDEPENDENT *Inquiry*

Have students develop their own rules and procedures for this activity. For example, have students decide which types of evidence are admissible in their "court." Encourage students to fully develop the courtroom scenario, using famous astronomers or other planets as "expert witnesses." Students could cross-examine witnesses, a "judge" could enforce rules of scientific evidence, and the jury could deliberate the case.

Quick Lab continued

Answer Key

5. Sample answer: I think that Pluto is a planet. Evidence that supports the idea that Pluto is a planet includes the fact that it orbits the sun, that it has a moon, and that it is larger than an asteroid. The fact that Pluto is very different from the other outer planets contradicts my opinion.

6. Sample answer: When Pluto was first discovered, scientists assumed it was a planet because it orbits the sun and because it moves in ways similar to how the other planets move. However, as scientists learned more about the solar system, Pluto's planetary status changed.

7. Sample answer: Scientists publish their findings in scientific journals for other scientists to review. They also make sure that scientific debates are based on evidence rather than on opinion. This helps to ensure that new evidence is evaluated based on its merits rather than on opinion.

Name ______________________ Class ______________ Date ______________

QUICK LAB GUIDED Inquiry

Pluto on Trial

In this lab, you will investigate how scientific descriptions of the solar system's structure have changed over time.

OBJECTIVES

- Describe evidence that supports or refutes Pluto's planetary status.
- Explain how scientific explanations change as new evidence is gathered.

MATERIALS

For each group

- chart paper
- markers
- research materials

PROCEDURE

1. Form two teams. One team should support the idea that Pluto is a planet. The other team should support the idea that Pluto is not a planet.
2. Work together as a team to develop your own definition of the term *planet*. This definition should support your claims about Pluto's planetary status.
3. Then, identify evidence to support your position using tables of planetary data in your textbook and additional **research materials**. Use the **chart paper** and **markers** to prepare illustrations to support your claims.
4. Hold a classroom trial to determine whether or not Pluto is a planet. Remember, teams must use evidence to support their claims.
5. After hearing the evidence, what is your opinion of Pluto's status? List three pieces of evidence that support your opinion. Is there any evidence that contradicts your opinion?

____

____

____

____

____

____

____

____

____

____

____

____

Quick Lab continued

6. Why did the scientific description of Pluto's status change over time?

7. During scientific investigations, scientists gather a wide variety of data about the natural world. Sometimes, scientists gather data that seem to contradict earlier explanations and theories. Describe two ways that scientists make sure that new evidence is discussed and debated.

QUICK LAB GUIDED Inquiry

Theory or Claim? GENERAL

Small groups
30 minutes

LAB RATINGS LESS ⟵⟶ MORE

Teacher Prep — 2
Student Setup — 1
Cleanup — 1

MATERIALS

For each group
- Internet access (optional)
- magazines
- newspapers
- other research materials
- paper, blank (1 sheet)

My Notes

SAFETY INFORMATION

Remind students to review all safety cautions and icons before beginning this lab.

TEACHER NOTES

In this activity, students compare the use of the word *theory* in science and in everyday life. For Step 2, provide each group with a short description of an ancient elemental "theory," such as the Greeks' Earth-Air-Fire-Water or the Chinese's Earth-Wood-Metal-Fire-Water.

You may need to provide specific resources for the student research in Step 3. This could include science-specific magazines or a list of science-based Internet sites. You may also need to provide a list of a few theories, such as plate tectonics, evolution, and nonscientific assertions that are not true scientific theories, such the geocentric view of the universe.

Skills Focus Conducting Research, Evaluating Information

MODIFICATION FOR INDEPENDENT Inquiry

Have each student group identify several processes that are always referred to as a "theory." Each group should make a hypothesis as to whether or not each item defines a scientific theory or just a claim and write a proposed procedure to test the hypothesis. Allow students to carry out any reasonable procedures. Encourage them to discuss with other groups their items, questions, hypotheses, procedures, and results.

Quick Lab continued

Answer Key

1. Sample answer: A theory is a well-supported and widely accepted explanation.
2. Accept all reasonable answers, but students' checklists should include items found in the formal definition of theory: reproducible, widely accepted, and well supported.
3. Sample answer: This is not a scientific theory. It is neither well supported nor widely accepted.
4. Sample answer: Theories: plate tectonics, dinosaur/meteor connection, evolution, big bang. Claims: UFOs, ghosts, Mayan 2012.
5. Answers may vary.
6. Sample answer: A scientific theory is not just a guess or one person's opinion. It is a widely accepted scientific view corroborated by experimentation.

Name _______________ Class _______________ Date _______________

QUICK LAB GUIDED *Inquiry*

Theory or Claim?

In this activity, you will determine the similarities and differences between a scientific theory and the word *theory* as used in common language. Once your determinations are complete, you will share your conclusions with the class.

OBJECTIVE

- Differentiate between a theory and a claim.

MATERIALS

For each group

- Internet access (optional)
- magazines
- newspapers
- other research materials
- paper, blank (1 sheet)

PROCEDURE

1. Work with your group to define the term *scientific theory*.

2. With your group, create a checklist of the characteristics of a scientific theory. Write your checklist on a piece of **blank paper**.

3. Your teacher will provide you with the wording of an assertion that is often referred to as a *theory* in the popular, nonscientific media. Investigate this statement. Apply your checklist to determine if it is a true scientific theory. Write your conclusion below.

Quick Lab continued

4. Through your own research, identify one additional scientific theory and one claim that you have heard called a theory, but that is not a scientific theory. Record your findings below.

5. Present your findings to the class. Create a list of all theories and claims presented by other groups. Use your checklist to decide whether you agree with their classifications. Record your conclusions below.

6. Describe two ways the word *theory* is used differently in science than in everyday life.

EXPLORATION LAB GUIDED Inquiry AND INDEPENDENT Inquiry

Science-Based Commercials GENERAL

Small groups
45 minutes

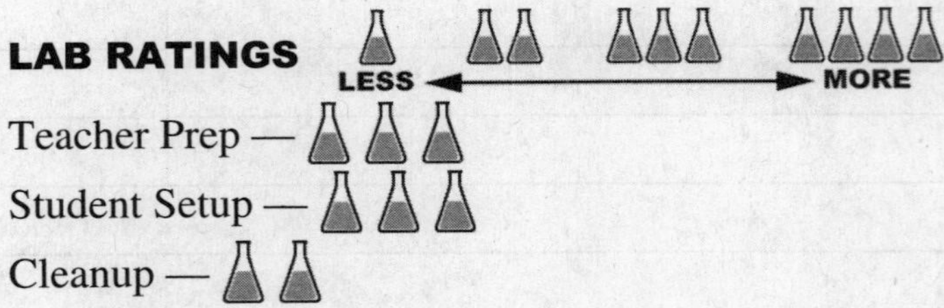

MATERIALS

For each group
- advertisements
- markers, colored
- paper, construction and white
- poster board (optional)
- scissors

SAFETY INFORMATION

Remind students to review all safety cautions and icons before beginning this lab.

TEACHER NOTES

In this lab, students will develop two commercials—one that uses scientific facts and one that uses pseudoscience—to support a product. Prior to the lab, clip ads from magazines or newspapers, print ads from Web sites, or write transcripts of television ads for students to evaluate before starting their own commercials. Alternatively, you may ask students to bring examples of ads that they think use science and pseudoscience.

Students will need to make up scientific facts to support their product, but they must be able to defend why the facts they use are scientifically valid. For example, they may say that their product improves test performance by 10%. This is not a scientific claim unless they tested many people, had a control group, and did not change any other variables while testing their product. Ask students to think of marketing claims they have seen or heard that use data to encourage consumers to buy products, with unacceptable scientific conclusions.

Skills Focus Developing Criteria, Examining Evidence, Drawing Conclusions

My Notes

MODIFICATION FOR DIRECTED Inquiry

Assign students specific products to advertise, and walk them through the steps of identifying scientific data, developing pseudoscientific claims, and incorporating that information into their advertisements. Give students examples of scientific and pseudoscientific information that they can use as a starting point for their advertisements.

Exploration Lab continued

Answer Key for GUIDED Inquiry

MAKE OBSERVATIONS

2. Answers will vary.

3. Answers will vary.

4. Sample answer: The claim in Step 2 seems to be based on experimental data; the one in Step 3 does not. The second ad also makes assumptions that may not be true.

DEVELOP A PLAN

5. Sample answer: My product is a sunscreen that turns pink when it is time to put on more sunscreen. It is called *Time's Up!*

6. Sample answer: When used as directed, our sunscreen prevented sunburn in 4 out 5 users.

7. Sample answer: Using *Time's Up!* sunscreen will make your skin younger.

9. Answers will vary.

ANALYZE THE RESULTS

10. Sample answer: Most classmates thought that the pseudoscientific claim was the most effective. I think the pseudoscientific claim was more effective because it sounded more definite.

DRAW CONCLUSIONS

11. Sample answer: The claim may or may not be scientific. The claim would be scientific if the tests were done on the product in the commercial, used proper scientific methods, and resulted in logical conclusions. They would not be scientific if scientific methods were not followed.

Connect TO THE ESSENTIAL QUESTION

12. Sample answer: To be scientific, the claim needed to be based on observations or experimental results, be testable by scientific methods, and be a logical conclusion based on data.

13. Sample answer: The claim is not scientific because although it is possible to test whether certain people think someone's skin *looks* younger, it is not possible for skin to actually *become* younger.

Exploration Lab continued

Answer Key for INDEPENDENT Inquiry

MAKE OBSERVATIONS

2. Answers will vary.
3. Answers will vary.
4. Sample answer: The claim in Step 2 seems to be based on experimental data; the one in Step 3 does not. The second ad also makes assumptions that may not be true.

DEVELOP A PLAN

5. Accept all reasonable answers.

ANALYZE THE RESULTS

8. Answers will vary.
9. Answers will vary.

DRAW CONCLUSIONS

10. Answers will vary.
11. Sample answer: The claim may or may not be scientific. The claim would be scientific if the tests were done on the product in the commercial, used proper scientific methods, and resulted in logical conclusions. They would not be scientific if scientific methods were not followed.

Connect TO THE ESSENTIAL QUESTION

12. Sample answer: To be scientific, the claim needed to be based on observations or experimental results, be testable by scientific methods, and be a logical conclusion based on data.
13. Sample answer: Pseudoscientific claims are not scientific because they use faulty logic, are not based on experiments and observations, or do not use scientific methods to obtain results.

Name ________________ Class ________ Date ________________

EXPLORATION LAB GUIDED *Inquiry*

Science-Based Commercials

In this activity, you will create two commercials for a product. One will use scientific facts, and the other will use pseudoscience to try to sell the product. Science has certain common characteristics. Not all scientific claims may be true, but they can be tested to determine if they are true. Pseudoscientific claims do not meet the same conditions as scientific claims.

OBJECTIVES

- Identify the characteristics of a scientific claim.
- Identify the characteristics of a pseudoscientific claim.

MATERIALS

For each group
- advertisements
- markers, colored
- paper, construction and white
- poster board (optional)
- scissors

PROCEDURE

MAKE OBSERVATIONS

1. Some advertisements present scientific information that makes products look favorable. Others present pseudoscience. Analyze the claims used in the **advertisements** your teacher gives you.

2. Identify one claim that seems to be based on science.

____

____

____

3. Identify one claim that seems to be based on pseudoscience.

____

____

____

4. How does the claim you listed in Step 2 differ from the one that you listed in Step 3?

____

____

____

____

____

DEVELOP A PLAN

5. Decide what type of product you will promote. What does it do? What is its name?

6. Imagine you have scientists at your company that can test the effectiveness of your product. They perform tests on your product. Describe some *scientific* results that could help you sell the product.

7. Now suppose that you did not do scientific studies to test your product or that the tests performed did not show that the product was better than similar products. What is a *pseudoscientific* claim you could use to promote your product?

8. On a separate sheet of **paper**, write scripts for two 30-second television commercials for your product. One commercial should use scientific results, and the other should use pseudoscientific claims. Use the available materials to design a package for your product that you can use in your commercial.

9. With your teacher's approval, perform your commercials for the class. Poll students to find out which commercial they thought was most effective. Do not tell the class which commercial was scientific and which was pseudoscientific.

   Science-based commercial ______________________

   Pseudoscience-based commercial ______________________

ANALYZE THE RESULTS

10. **Analyzing Results** Which of your claims was the most effective? Why do you think this claim was more effective than the other claim?

DRAW CONCLUSIONS

11. **Applying Concepts** Some commercials reference test results that they say support their products. Do you think that the claim must be true because it is based on scientific evidence? Explain your reasoning.

Connect TO THE ESSENTIAL QUESTION

12. **Analyzing Criteria** What criteria did you use to determine whether a claim is scientific?

13. **Explaining Criteria** Why isn't the pseudoscientific claim that you developed science?

Name ______________________ Class ____________ Date ______________

EXPLORATION LAB INDEPENDENT Inquiry

Science-Based Commercials

In this activity, you will explore how science and pseudoscience are used to sell products. Science has certain common characteristics. Not all scientific claims may be true, but they can be tested to determine if they are true. Pseudoscientific claims do not meet the same conditions as scientific claims.

OBJECTIVES

- Identify the characteristics of a scientific claim.
- Identify the characteristics of a pseudoscientific claim.

MATERIALS

For each group

- advertisements
- markers, colored
- paper, construction and white
- poster board (optional)
- scissors

PROCEDURE

RESEARCH A PROBLEM

1. Use the **advertisements** your teacher gives you to research how science and pseudoscience are used to sell products.

MAKE OBSERVATIONS

2. Identify one claim used in advertising that seems to be based on science.

____

____

____

3. Identify one claim used in advertising that seems to be based on pseudoscience.

____

____

____

4. How does the claim you listed in Step 2 differ from the one that you listed in Step 3?

____

____

____

____

DEVELOP A PLAN

5. Explain how you could make commercials that use scientific and pseudoscientific claims for the class to evaluate.

6. On a separate sheet of **paper**, write the steps to your plan. Include a materials list, if needed. Explain how you will determine if you were effective in presenting how science differs from pseudoscience.

7. After your teacher approves your plan, present your commercials to the class.

ANALYZE THE RESULTS

8. **Defending Results** How did you use scientific claims in your commercials? Why are these claims considered to be science?

9. **Developing Conclusions** When you watched other students, were you able to tell which claims were scientific and which were pseudoscientific? Explain.

DRAW CONCLUSIONS

10 **Analyzing Methods** Explain whether your commercials were effective in presenting the difference between science and pseudoscience.

11 **Applying Concepts** Some commercials reference test results that they say support their products. Do you think that the claim must be true because it is based on scientific evidence? Explain your reasoning.

Connect TO THE ESSENTIAL QUESTION

12 **Analyzing Criteria** What criteria did you use to determine whether a claim is scientific?

13 **Explaining Criteria** What evidence can you use to determine whether a claim is pseudoscientific?

QUICK LAB GUIDED *Inquiry*

Which Scientist Am I? BASIC

Small groups
20 minutes/day for 2 days

LAB RATINGS LESS ⟷ MORE

Teacher Prep — 1
Student Setup — 1
Cleanup — 1

MATERIALS

For each group
- heavyweight white paper, 4.25" × 5.5"
- pencils

For the whole class
- number cube with 5 squares labeled "Ask" and one square labeled "Guess"

SAFETY INFORMATION

Remind students to review all safety cautions and icons before beginning this lab.

TEACHER NOTES

In this activity, students will create and play a guessing game to learn more about scientists from diverse backgrounds. Provide students with a list of scientists from diverse backgrounds, such as Subrahmanyan Chandrasekhar, Jewel Plummer Cobb, Marie Maynard Daly, Albert Einstein, Stephen Hawking, Shirley Ann Jackson, Lydia Villa-Komaroff, Samuel Lee Kountz, Jr., Eloy Rodriguez, and Jane Cooke Wright.

Have each student group choose a different scientist to research. Guide students in asking and researching questions about the scientist's life. Have students create a card for each scientist that contains a short summary of the scientist's background and major works. On the next day, have students play "Which Scientist Am I?" Collect each group's card. One player chooses and reads a card. The remaining players take turns rolling the game cube and either asking one question about the scientist or guessing the identity of the scientist.

Skills Focus Conducting Research, Summarizing Information

My Notes

MODIFICATION FOR INDEPENDENT *Inquiry*

Have students research a scientist of their own choosing and create a poster about the scientist's background and major works to display in the classroom.

Answer Key

3. Answers will vary.

4. Answers will vary.

Name ______________________ Class ______________ Date ______________

QUICK LAB GUIDED *Inquiry*

Which Scientist Am I?

The body of scientific knowledge is built and advanced by the works of scientists from all kinds of backgrounds. In this lab, you will create and play a game to learn more about the diverse backgrounds of scientists.

OBJECTIVE

- Explain that scientists who make contributions to scientific knowledge come from all kinds of backgrounds.

MATERIALS

For each group

- heavyweight white paper, 4.25" × 5.5"
- pencils

For the whole class

- number cube with 5 squares labeled "Ask" and one square labeled "Guess"

PROCEDURE

1. Working as a group, choose a scientist from the list provided by your teacher. Write the name of your scientist below.

   ____

2. Use the Internet or library resources to learn more about the life and work of your scientist. Take notes in the space below or in your notebook. Make sure to note your sources.

   ____
   ____
   ____
   ____
   ____
   ____
   ____
   ____

3. Describe the background of your scientist. Include information about where the scientist was born and grew up, and the scientist's childhood and education.

   ____
   ____
   ____
   ____
   ____
   ____
   ____
   ____

Quick Lab continued

4. Summarize the major scientific work of your scientist. Include information about where the scientist was or is employed; what discoveries, theories, or inventions the scientist produced; and any major awards the scientist won.

5. Create a card for your scientist on the paper your teacher has provided. Write the name of your scientist on top of the card. Use the information from Steps 3 and 4 to write a short summary of your scientist's background and major contributions to scientific knowledge. When the whole class has created their cards, you will play a game in which you try to guess the identity of each scientist based on his or her characteristics. In the space below, record the major accomplishments of the different scientists your classmates studied.

QUICK LAB INDEPENDENT *Inquiry*

Design a Game About Goals GENERAL

Small groups

20 minutes, plus an optional 20 minutes on a second day

LAB RATINGS LESS ↔ MORE

Teacher Prep — 2

Student Setup — 2

Cleanup — 2

MATERIALS

For each group
- cardboard or blank game board
- construction paper
- glue
- number cube
- markers
- pencils
- poster board

SAFETY INFORMATION

Remind students to review all safety cautions and icons before beginning this lab.

TEACHER NOTES

In this activity, students will design a game to learn about the various goals that drive the work of scientists. Guide the class in brainstorming a list of ideas about why scientists conduct investigations. Then, have students work in small groups to discuss how each goal on the list may affect scientists and their work. Students should discuss their answers to the questions in the lab procedure. Provide students with materials to design their own game based on the goals of scientists. If time permits on another day, have students play each other's games.

Skills Focus Brainstorming, Ideas Evaluating Ideas

My Notes

MODIFICATION FOR DIRECTED *Inquiry*

Create a board game as a whole group. Create a game board with 15–20 spaces. Write, "Pick a Goal Card" on 5 of the spaces. Create a set of goal cards, each with a different goal from the brainstorm list. Ask students to vote on whether picking the goal should allow the player to progress 3 steps, stay at the same position, or go back 3 steps, and write the result on the card. If desired, guide students in developing game elements for other spaces. Players advance through the game by rolling a number cube.

Quick Lab continued

Answer Key

2. Examples of admirable goals may include finding cures for diseases; helping people meet basic needs for food, clean water, and clean air; and creating technologies to make work easier. Examples of goals that may raise ethical questions include making a lot of money; becoming famous for inventing or discovering something; and valuing technology over humans.

3. Examples of how life experiences may affect the goals of scientists may include wanting to cure diseases that family members suffer from; wanting to improve poor environmental conditions experienced during childhood; and dreaming of traveling in space or other inspirations from media. Students should explain that it is important for people of diverse life experiences to become scientists because a diversity of goals allows many different avenues of science to advance.

Name ______________________ Class ______________ Date ____________________

QUICK LAB INDEPENDENT *Inquiry*

Design a Game About Goals

In this lab, you will learn about the goals that drive scientists and their work. Goals include the objectives of specific investigations, as well as greater intentions that drive a scientist's career and sense of life purpose. Goals are often shaped by life experiences. In turn, the goals of scientists drive the progress of science.

After brainstorming and discussing goals, you will work with a group to design a game based on the theme of goals.

OBJECTIVE

- Describe how scientists from different backgrounds contribute to science.

MATERIALS

For each group

- cardboard or blank game board
- construction paper
- glue
- number cube
- markers
- pencils
- poster board

PROCEDURE

1. As a class, brainstorm ideas about why scientists conduct investigations. Come up with a list of goals that may drive different scientists and their work.
2. Do some goals on the list seem to have more merit than others? Do any goals on the list raise ethical problems? Write your ideas about the merits of different goals on the lines below.

3. How does the life experience of a scientist affect his or her goals? Why is it important for people of diverse backgrounds and life experiences to become scientists? Explain your ideas on the lines below.

___

___

___

___

___

___

___

___

___

___

___

___

___

4. Discuss your responses to the questions above with your group.
5. Your teacher will distribute **materials** to your group. Use the materials, and your ideas about the goals that drive scientists and their work, to create a game with the theme of goals.
6. If time permits, play your game as a group, and share your game with other groups. Play the games that other groups have created.

QUICK LAB DIRECTED Inquiry

Heart Rate and Exercise GENERAL

Small groups
30 minutes

LAB RATINGS

LESS ← → MORE

Teacher Prep —
Student Setup —
Cleanup —

MATERIALS

For each group
- calculator (optional)
- paper, graph (1 sheet)
- pencil
- stopwatch

My Notes

SAFETY INFORMATION

Remind students to review all safety cautions and icons before beginning this lab. Students with cardiovascular or respiratory illnesses should not act as subjects. Because subjects should be able to run in place for five minutes, it is important to know if students have any limitations. Be sensitive to medical conditions, body weight issues, or other personal issues that would make a student uncomfortable volunteering to be a subject. If any subject's heart rate rises above 180 beats per minute, or if a subject feels faint, dizzy, or otherwise ill, he or she should stop running immediately.

TEACHER NOTES

In this lab, students will study the effects of exercise on heart rate. Groups should consist of three students. Instruct students how to find a pulse on the inner side of the wrist under the thumb. Students should practice the technique before undertaking the activity. Students should count beats for 15 seconds and then multiply by 4 to get beats per minute.

Skills Focus Collecting Data, Constructing Graphs, Comparing Results

MODIFICATION FOR INDEPENDENT Inquiry

Have students identify and investigate factors that affect heart rate. They should identify a testable question and propose an investigation that will allow them to answer their question. Allow students to carry out all reasonable procedures. Students should share their results with the class.

Answer Key

2. Answers will vary.

3. Answers will vary.

4. Answers will vary.

Quick Lab continued

5. Answers will vary.
6. Sample answer: The heart rate was lowest at 0 minutes. It increased steadily for the first 2 minutes and then leveled off until the subject stopped running. When the subject stopped running, the heart rate slowly returned to its initial level.
7. Sample answer: Other subjects had different actual heart rates, but the general shape of the curve was the same for all groups.
8. Sample answer: The physical fitness of the subjects, the accuracy of the data collector, and the speed at which the subjects ran may all have affected the results.

Name ______________________ Class ______________ Date ______________

QUICK LAB DIRECTED Inquiry

Heart Rate and Exercise

In this lab, you will determine how heart rate varies with exercise.

PROCEDURE

1. Identify one person in your group to be the subject, one person to be the data collector, and one person to be the recorder.

2. The data collector should determine the heart rate of the subject while the subject is standing still (at rest). The recorder should record the heart rate in the table below.

Time (min)	Heart rate (beats per minute)	Time (min)	Heart rate (beats per minute)
0 (at rest)		5 (running)	
1 (running)		6 (at rest)	
2 (running)		7 (at rest)	
3 (running)		8 (at rest)	
4 (running)		9 (at rest)	

3. The recorder should start the **stopwatch**. The subject should run in place as fast as possible for 5 minutes. Each minute, the data collector should measure the subject's heart rate, and the recorder should record it in the table.

4. The subject should stop running. Each minute for 4 minutes, the data collector should measure the heart rate, and the recorder should record it in the table.

5. Make a line graph of the subject's heart rate on a piece of **graph paper**.

OBJECTIVES

- Describe how exercise affects heart rate.
- Identify patterns in data.

MATERIALS

For each group

- calculator (optional)
- paper, graph (1 sheet)
- pencil
- stopwatch

Quick Lab continued

6. What pattern do the data show?

7. How do your group's data compare with the data of the other groups?

8. What factors may have caused any differences among groups' data sets?

QUICK LAB DIRECTED *Inquiry*

Modeling Heights of Students GENERAL

Individual student
30 minutes

LAB RATINGS LESS ⟵⟶ MORE

Teacher Prep — 2
Student Setup — 1
Cleanup — 2

MATERIALS

For each student
- notebook
- paper, graphing

For the class
- tape measure

My Notes

SAFETY INFORMATION

Remind students to review all safety cautions and icons before beginning this lab. Students will measure each other's height. Remind students to be respectful of other students.

TEACHER NOTES

In this activity, students represent human height using a mathematical model. Using all of the people in the class, students divide individuals into groups (male, female, age groups, and so on). They then measure everyone's height and tabulate the data. Finally, they create a bar graph to show how different groups segregate into different size categories (for example, girls versus boys, youngest versus oldest). If a measuring tape is not available, then a meter stick can be used to measure the students' height.

Tip This activity will demonstrate that any group of objects or people can be modeled mathematically.

Skills Focus Practicing Lab Techniques, Tabulating Data, Making Graphs

MODIFICATION FOR GUIDED *Inquiry*

Have students determine the best way to group the height data and create their own data tables.

Quick Lab continued

Answer Key

5. Accept all reasonable answers. Sample data:

STUDENT HEIGHT

Student name	Gender	Height (cm)
Jim	m	157
Aliyah	f	158
John	m	160
Abigail	f	145
James	m	185
Agnes	f	175
Jerome	m	164
Ansel	m	152
Joanne	f	142
Andy	m	177

6. Accept all reasonable answers. Sample answer from the table = 185–142 = 43 cm.

7. Accept all reasonable answers. Sample answer:

STUDENT HEIGHT ARRANGED FROM LOWEST TO HIGHEST

Student	Height (cm)
Joanne	142
Abigail	145
Ansel	152
Jim	157
Aliyah	158
John	160
Jerome	164
Agnes	175
Andy	177
James	185

Quick Lab continued

8. Accept all reasonable answers. Sample answer:

GROUPED STUDENT HEIGHTS

Increment	Numbers within this range
141–150	2
151–160	4
161–170	1
171–180	2
181–190	1

9. Accept all reasonable answers. Sample answer:

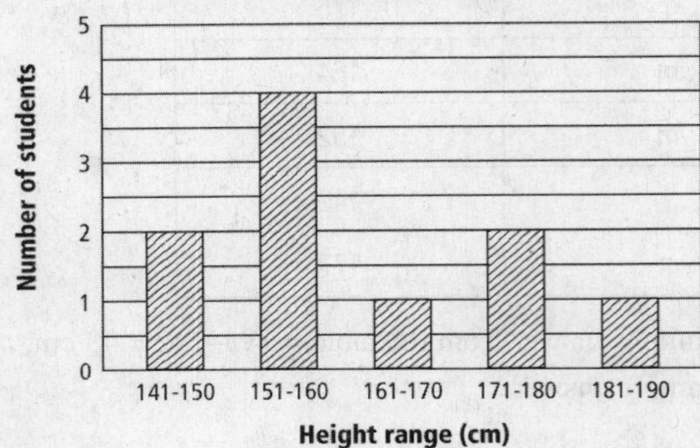

10. Accept all reasonable answers.
Teacher prompt Do you see a height range that contains more students than others?

11. Accept all reasonable answers.
Teacher prompt Do you see a difference between boys' heights and girls' heights?

Name ______________________ Class ______________ Date ______________

QUICK LAB DIRECTED Inquiry

Modeling Heights of Students

In this lab you will measure the heights of fellow students and model the data using bar graphs.

PROCEDURE

1. Select a suitable wall, chalkboard, whiteboard, or vertical surface on which marks can be made.
2. For each student, ensure he or she stands straight, back to the wall or surface.
3. Make a mark at a point level with the top of the head.
4. Use the tape measure to measure the distance from the mark to the ground.
5. Repeat Steps 1 to 4 for each student. Write your data in the table provided (add more rows if needed).

OBJECTIVE

- Measure student heights and use a graph to highlight individual and group characteristics.

MATERIALS

For each student

- notebook
- paper, graphing

For the class

- tape measure

STUDENT HEIGHT

Student name	Gender	Height (cm)

6 The maximum and minimum heights represent the range of the data. What is the range?

____

7 Organize the data from minimum to maximum height so that minimum is at the top of the column and maximum is at the bottom.

STUDENT HEIGHT ARRANGED FROM LOWEST TO HIGHEST

Student name	Height (cm)

8 Divide the range by a suitable factor, such as 5, and create another table with increments of each factor, starting with the minimum. Count how many height measurements are within each increment, and enter the data in the following table. You may have to experiment with using different factors so that you end up with at least 5 or 6 increments.

GROUPED STUDENT HEIGHTS

Increment	Numbers within this range

Name ______________________ Class ______________ Date ______________

Quick Lab continued

9. Create a bar graph to present the number of students in each of the increments of height.

10. What do you notice about the data when you examine your graph?

____

____

____

____

____

11. Repeat Steps 8 to 9 with the data separated into two groups: girls and boys. Draw a new bar graph based on this grouping. What do you notice about the data when you examine this graph?

____

____

____

____

____

FIELD LAB GUIDED *Inquiry* **AND** INDEPENDENT *Inquiry*

Investigate Water Usage GENERAL

Small groups

Two 45-minute class periods

MATERIALS

For each group
- calculator
- notebook

LAB RATINGS

LESS ◄——► MORE

Teacher Prep — 1

Student Setup — 2

Cleanup — 1

My Notes

SAFETY INFORMATION

Remind students to review all safety cautions and icons before beginning this lab. Students may have to interact with strangers. Emphasize the need for caution and common sense when interacting with strangers.

TEACHER NOTES

In this activity, students collect and compare data on water usage in a home and in a business. They develop data collection and tabulation methods and use home water use data to estimate daily water usage. For the field part of the lab, students find a local business and request an interview of the facilities manager. (The school custodian is acceptable if no local business is available.) Students should be briefed on interviewing techniques and courtesy, and what to reasonably expect when interviewing a stranger. During the interview, students will obtain information on all the ways the business uses water in a day. This information is tabulated and compared with the information on home water use. Finally, students are asked to identify ways in which water use can be reduced in homes and in businesses.

You may wish to hold a class discussion at the beginning of this lab to talk about methods for collecting data on water use. The aim should be to estimate water volumes based on typical use. This could include timing an activity and collecting water for that amount of time to estimate the volume of water used. Measurements for flushing a toilet can be estimated from the size of the toilet reservoir. The amount of water used for laundry can be found from the specification sheet for a particular model of washing machine, usually available online. Another option is to have students take readings from a water meter or from a water bill.

Tip This activity will help students learn how to tabulate data in a way that allows information to be easily compared.

Student Tip Construct your tables to allow easy comparison of data.

Skills Focus Collecting Data, Tabulating Data, Evaluating Data

MODIFICATION FOR DIRECTED *Inquiry*

For the directed inquiry level option, provide students with data tables that you construct ahead of time.

Field Lab continued

Answer Key for GUIDED *Inquiry*

MAKE OBSERVATIONS

2. Accept all reasonable answers.

4. Sample data for a three-person household:

HOME WATER USAGE

Activity	Amount of water per use (liters)	Number of uses per day	Amount used per week (liters)
flushing toilet	12	12	144
taking a shower	75	3	225
taking a bath	150	1	150
running clothes washer	120	1	120
running dishwasher	70	1	70
running kitchen faucet	8	7	56
brushing teeth	5	6	30
		Total weekly usage	795

6. Sample data for a five-employee business:

BUSINESS WATER USAGE

Activity	Amount of water per use (liters)	Number of uses per day	Amount used per week (liters)
flushing toilets	6	60	360
running kitchen faucet	8	5	40
washing products	2	550	1100
watering lawn	150	1	150
		Total weekly usage	1650

Field Lab continued

ANALYZE THE RESULTS

7. Accept all reasonable answers.
   Teacher prompt Which activity shows the highest value in the weekly amount column?
8. Accept all reasonable answers.
   Teacher prompt Which activity shows the highest value in the weekly amount column?

DRAW CONCLUSIONS

9. Sample answer: Use a low-flush toilet and a low-flow shower head. Take showers instead of baths. Run the washing machine or dishwasher only when there is a full load. Turn off the faucet while brushing teeth.
   Teacher prompt How might you modify or change the activities that use large amounts of water?
10. Sample answer: Water the lawn every other day instead of once a day. Look for ways to reduce water in industrial processes.
    Teacher prompt How might you modify or change the activities at the business that used the most water?

Connect TO THE ESSENTIAL QUESTION

11. Sample answer: The tables are constructed in the same way, using the same columns, which makes the data easy to compare.

Answer Key for INDEPENDENT Inquiry

DEVELOP A PLAN

2. Sample answer: The aim is to estimate water usage based on typical use. This could include timing an activity and collecting water for that amount of time to estimate the volume of water used.
   Teacher prompt How do you measure an amount of water?
3. Sample answer: Since we can't directly measure the amount of water a business uses, the best way is to ask the person in charge.
   Teacher prompt Who might have the information you are looking for?

Field Lab continued

MAKE OBSERVATIONS

5. Sample answer for a three-person household:

HOME WATER USAGE

Activity	Amount of water per use (liters)	Number of uses per day	Amount used per week (liters)
flushing toilet	12	12	144
taking a shower	75	3	225
taking a bath	150	1	150
running clothes washer	120	1	120
running dishwasher	70	1	70
running kitchen faucet	8	7	56
brushing teeth	5	6	30
		Total weekly usage	795

BUSINESS WATER USAGE

Activity	Amount of water per use (liters)	Number of uses per day	Amount used per week (liters)
flushing toilets	6	60	360
running kitchen faucet	8	5	40
washing products	2	550	1100
watering lawn	150	1	150
		Total weekly usage	1650

ANALYZE THE RESULTS

6. Accept all reasonable answers.
Teacher prompt Which activity shows the highest value in the weekly amount column?

Field Lab continued

7. Accept all reasonable answers.
   Teacher prompt Which activity shows the highest value in the weekly amount column?

DRAW CONCLUSIONS

8. Sample answer: Use a low-flush toilet or a low-flow shower head. Take showers instead of baths. Run the washing machine or dishwasher only when there is a full load. Turn off the faucet while brushing teeth.
   Teacher prompt How might you modify or change the activities that use large amounts of water?
9. Sample answer: Water the lawn every other day instead of once a day. Look for ways to reduce water in industrial processes.
   Teacher prompt How might you modify or change the activities at the business that used the most water?

Connect TO THE ESSENTIAL QUESTION

10. Sample answer: The tables are constructed in the same way, using the same columns, which makes the data easy to compare.

Name ______________________ Class ______________ Date ______________

FIELD LAB GUIDED *Inquiry*

Investigate Water Use

In this activity, you will collect and compare water use data from a home and a business.

OBJECTIVE

- Compare the amounts of water used in a home to the amounts of water used by a business.

MATERIALS

For each group

- calculator
- notebook

PROCEDURE

ASK A QUESTION

1. Water is an essential resource used by people in both homes and businesses. Some businesses also use water for industrial processes. The question you will be exploring in this lab is: How does water use in a home differ from that in a business?

MAKE OBSERVATIONS

2. Write down all the ways you use water in a day. Start with the time you get up in the morning. Include things such as brushing your teeth, flushing the toilet, using ice, and taking a shower. Make a table in your notebook to keep track of this information. Use the one shown below or create your own.

HOME WATER USAGE

Use of water	Amount of water per use	Number of uses per day	Amount used per week
		Total weekly usage	

3. For each use of water, estimate the amount of water used for each activity. This could include timing an activity and collecting water for that amount of time to estimate the volume of water used. Total the amount for all activities.

Field Lab continued

4. Add up how many liters of water your household uses in a day, and multiply that by 7. This is how much water you use in a week.

5. For the field part of the lab, find a local business and request an interview with the facilities manager. (The school custodian is acceptable if no local business is available.)

6. Obtain information on all the ways the business uses water in a day. Make a table in your notebook to record this information.

ANALYZE THE RESULTS

7. **Comparing Data** Which of your activities at home used the greatest volume of water?

____

8. **Comparing Data** Which business activity used the greatest volume of water?

____

DRAW CONCLUSIONS

9. **Evaluating Results** What are some ways that you could reduce your water use?

____

____

____

____

____

10. **Evaluating Results** What are some ways that the business could reduce its water use?

____

____

____

____

____

Name ______________________ Class ______________ Date ______________

Field Lab continued

Connect TO THE ESSENTIAL QUESTION

11 **Explaining Concepts** How does the tabulation of data allow you to easily compare water use in a home to water use in a business?

____

____

____

____

Name ______________________ Class ____________ Date ______________

FIELD LAB INDEPENDENT Inquiry

Investigate Water Use

In this activity, you will collect and compare water use data from a home and a business.

OBJECTIVE

- Compare the amounts of water used in a home to the amounts of water used by a business.

MATERIALS

For each group

- calculator
- notebook

PROCEDURE

ASK A QUESTION

1. Water is an essential resource used by people in both homes and businesses. Some businesses also use water for industrial processes. The question you will be exploring in this lab is: How does water use in a home differ from that in a business?

DEVELOP A PLAN

2. Consider how to collect data on domestic water use. Your own home may be typical. How will you collect data on water use at your home?

____

____

____

3. Consider how to collect data on business water use. How will you collect data on water use at a business?

____

____

____

MAKE OBSERVATIONS

4. In your notebook, create two tables, one to record home water use and another to record business water use. Each table should include a way to record the types of activities that use water, the amount of water used in each activity, the number of uses per day, the amount used per week, and total weekly water use.

5. Collect data according to your plans from Steps 2 and 3 above.

ANALYZE THE RESULTS

6. **Comparing Data** Which of your activities at home used the greatest volume of water?

____

Name ______________________ Class ____________ Date ______________

Field Lab continued

7 **Comparing Data** Which business activity used the greatest volume of water?

____

DRAW CONCLUSIONS

8 **Evaluating Results** What are some ways that you could reduce your water use?

____

____

____

9 **Evaluating Results** What are some ways that the business could reduce its water use?

____

____

____

Connect TO THE ESSENTIAL QUESTION

10 **Explaining Concepts** How does the tabulation of data allow you to easily compare water use in a home to water use in a business?

____

____

____

____

QUICK LAB DIRECTED *Inquiry*

Investigate Making Measurements GENERAL

Student pairs
25 minutes

MATERIALS

For each pair

- classroom objects, similar length (5)
- ruler, metric

My Notes

LAB RATINGS

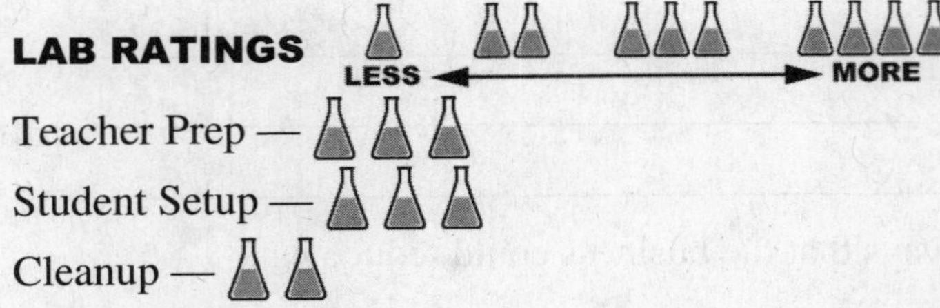

Teacher Prep —
Student Setup —
Cleanup —

SAFETY INFORMATION

Remind students to review all safety cautions and icons before beginning this lab.

TEACHER NOTES

In this activity, students work in pairs to construct a ruler using their own system of units. Then they will measure the lengths of five classroom objects of their choice using their ruler. During the data collection phase of the lab, students will have to make a decision about how to make their measurements—should they use whole numbers or should they make estimates of the decimal values of their units? Allow students to make this decision themselves. Students will also compare their results for the five objects to get an idea of variation in measurements. Students will also compare their ruler with a metric ruler, determine a conversion factor, and convert length in their units to the SI unit of meters.

Tip This activity will help students gain experience with making measurements and with converting measurements from one unit to another.

Student Tip How do you decide how many decimal places to use when you make a measurement? Try to estimate to the nearest 0.1 unit of the smallest marked unit on a measuring tool.

Skills Focus Practicing Lab Techniques, Recording Data, Making Conversions

MODIFICATION FOR GUIDED *Inquiry*

Allow students to study the empty grid and to think about how they could use it to make a ruler from scratch. Then have them make their ruler and use it to measure five objects, constructing their own table for keeping track of their measurements.

Quick Lab continued

Answer Key

2. Sample answer:

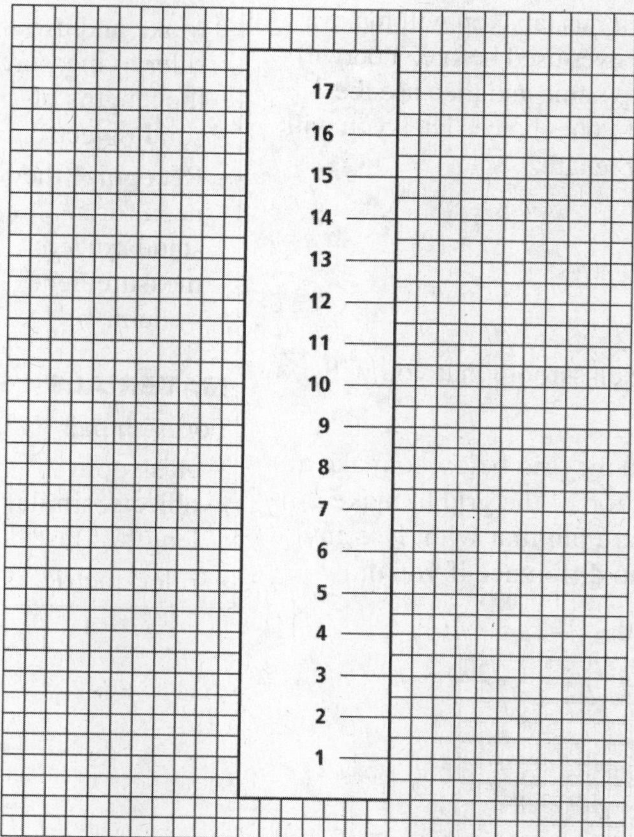

3. Accept all reasonable answers.

5. Accept all reasonable answers.

6. The objects will not have lengths that correspond to exactly one whole number values of their made-up units. Students should realize that they will have to go one decimal place beyond their marked unit values in making length measurements.

7. Check student calculations to be sure the conversion factors are calculated correctly.

8. Check student calculations to be sure averages are calculated correctly.

9. Sample answer: We could use a metric ruler to measure the object and compare this to our calculated value.

10. Accept all reasonable answers. Students should be able to see that there is a range of values.

11. Sample answer: It is important to have standardized units so that everyone can easily compare their measurements. If all measurements use different units, it is hard to compare and communicate results.

Name ______________________ Class ______________ Date ______________

QUICK LAB DIRECTED *Inquiry*

Investigate Making Measurements

Whenever you want to measure the length, width, or height of an object, you reach for a ruler marked off in centimeters or in inches. But, is it possible to use some other unit of measure? In this lab, you will make a ruler composed of a new unit that no one has ever used before. You will name these new units with your own made-up name and then use the ruler to measure the lengths of five objects of your choice. Then you will convert these measurements to the SI unit for length.

OBJECTIVES

- Make and use a ruler to measure the lengths of solid objects.
- Recognize the need for a standardized measurement system.

MATERIALS

For each pair

- classroom objects, similar length (5)
- ruler, metric

PROCEDURE

1. As a class, choose five objects in the classroom that you will measure.
2. With your partner, decide how to use the grid below to make a ruler. Draw a long, thin rectangle on top of the grid to make a final shape similar to the rulers you are familiar with. Use any part of the grid to do this. It makes no difference if you draw your ruler horizontally or vertically.

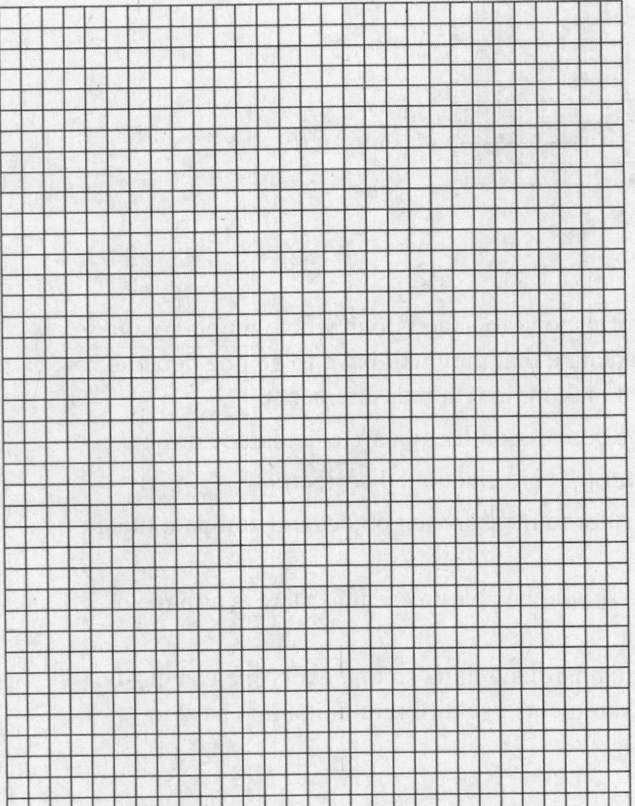

Name ______________________ Class ______________ Date ______________

Quick Lab continued

❸ Mark off your ruler in units of your choice. You do not need to use every grid line, but use some whole number grouping of grid lines to represent individual repeating units on your ruler. For example, you might use two gridlines to represent one unit. In this case, you would make a mark at every other gridline along the length of your ruler.

❹ Decide on a name for your units.

____

❺ Use your ruler to measure the long side of each of the five objects in your made-up units. Be sure that each group measures the same side of the objects so that you can compare your results later. Record your data in the table below. Be sure to also write down the name of the units you used to make the measurements.

OBJECT LENGTH DATA

Name of object	Length in ______ units

❻ Did your measurements reveal that the objects you measured were exactly some whole number value of your units or did you have to make an estimate of a fractional portion of your unit to make an accurate measurement? How did you decide what type of number (whole number or decimal number) to record in the table?

____

____

____

❼ Use a metric ruler to determine how many of your units are equivalent to 5 centimeters (cm). Do this by laying a metric ruler parallel to your ruler and counting the number of your units that cover the same length as 5 cm. Divide 5.0 cm by that number of your units to obtain a conversion factor.

____

Name ______________________ Class ______________ Date ______________

Quick Lab continued

8 Convert the average length in your units to the average length in centimeters using your conversion factor. Then convert the average in centimeters to the average in meters. Show your work.

9 How could you test to see if your calculation in Step 8 was correct?

____

____

10 Compare the SI value of your unit with the other groups. How did their measurements differ from yours?

____

____

____

11 Why is it important to have a standardized measurement system?

____

____

____

QUICK LAB GUIDED Inquiry

Investigating Density GENERAL

Student pairs
30 minutes

LAB RATINGS LESS ⟷ MORE

Teacher Prep — 4
Student Setup — 3
Cleanup — 3

MATERIALS

For each pair
- balance
- cylinder, graduated, 100 mL
- ruler, metric
- solid of known density (cube)
- water

For each student
- lab apron
- safety goggles

My Notes

SAFETY INFORMATION

Remind students to review all safety cautions and icons before beginning this lab. To avoid cracking the glass cylinder, caution students not to drop the solid into the graduated cylinders. Rather, have them tilt the cylinder and then gently slide the solid into it. Be sure students do not spill any water from the cylinder as they tilt it.

TEACHER NOTES

In this activity, students determine the density of a solid. The students measure the mass of their solid using a balance. They calculate the volume two ways: from linear measurements they make using a ruler and from measurements they make using water displacement. Students will compare their volume calculations resulting from the two methods and use them to calculate density. They will get an idea of the precision of their density values by comparing density results with other groups to see how they vary. Students will wrap up by comparing their density results with the known density of the solid to determine accuracy.

Provide the same solid to all groups. This solid must have a density greater than 1.0 g/cm^3 so that the water displacement steps can be carried out. The solid must also be of a size to fit into a 100-mL graduated cylinder. Examples include sugar cubes, rock candy (roughly cubic), or modeling clay shaped into a small cube.

Tip This activity will help students identify units of mass and volume and the tools used to make those measurements

Student Tip Why might there be variation in measurements?

Skills Focus Practicing Lab Techniques, Comparing Results, Identifying Variation

MODIFICATION FOR GUIDED Inquiry

For the Guided Inquiry option of this activity, student can be challenged to assess the accuracy of estimating density with the provided materials.

Quick Lab continued

Answer Key

6. Sample answer: Human error when reading the measurements may account for some of the difference in these values.
8. Sample answer: Our measurements of density were similar to those of others in the class, but not exactly the same. Some people may read the ruler or the markings on the graduated cylinder in a different way than other people read them.
   Teacher Prompt Does everyone read measurements in exactly the same way?
9. Our measurements of density were similar to the known density, but not exactly the same. We might have allowed some water to splash out of the graduated cylinder by accident, which would have made our volume for the solid too low.

Name ______________________ Class ______________ Date ______________

QUICK LAB GUIDED *Inquiry*

Investigating Density

In this lab you will make measurements of physical properties of an object and use those measurements to determine the density of the object. You will compare the results to see how measurements can vary depending on the tools used to make them. You will also be able to compare your results with other groups in your class to see how they vary across several trials. Finally, you will compare your results with the known density of the object to determine how accurately you calculated the density of the object.

OBJECTIVES

- Determine the density of a solid using two methods for volume determination.
- Compare results with those of other class members to evaluate precision.
- Compare results with the known density of the solid to evaluate accuracy.

MATERIALS

For each pair
- balance
- cylinder, graduated, 100 mL
- solid of known density (cube)
- ruler, metric
- water

For each student
- lab apron
- safety goggles

PROCEDURE

1. Your teacher will provide you with a solid. Use the balance to determine its mass and record this information in the table below.

PHYSICAL MEASUREMENTS OF SOLID

				Water displacement	
Mass (g)	Length (cm)	Width (cm)	Height (cm)	Volume of water before adding the solid (mL)	Volume of water after adding the solid (mL)

2. Use the ruler to measure the solid's length, width, and height to the nearest millimeter (0.1 cm). Record your data in the data table above.

3. Add enough water to the graduated cylinder to fill it about halfway. Record the water volume to the nearest milliliter (mL) in the data table above.

4. Carefully slide the solid into the graduated cylinder so that no water splashes out. Read and record the combined volume of the water and solid. Record this volume in the data table above.

5. Calculate the volume of the solid using the linear dimensions that you measured with the ruler. Then calculate the volume of the solid using the water displacement data. Record your results in the table on the next page.

Name ______________________ Class ______________ Date ______________

Quick Lab continued

VOLUME OF SOLID

Volume from linear measurements (cm^3)	Volume from water displacement (mL)

6 One mL is equivalent to one cubic centimeter in volume. With this in mind, how do the two volumes in the table compare? Are the volumes the same? If not, what might account for any differences?

____

____

____

7 Use each calculated volume from the table above to determine the density of the solid in grams per cubic centimeter (g/cm^3). Solid densities are generally expressed in g/cm^3 so you can convert mL to cm^3 for the water displacement value.

DENSITY OF SOLID

Density using volume from linear measurements (g/cm^3)	Density using volume from water displacement (g/cm^3)

8 Compare your results with those of other groups in your class. How similar are your density values to those of your classmates? What might account for any differences?

____

____

____

9 Ask your teacher to tell you the known density of your solid. Compare your density results with the known density. How similar are each of your two density results to the known density? What might account for any differences?

____

____

____

FIELD LAB DIRECTED Inquiry **AND** GUIDED Inquiry

Use a Sextant to Make a Map GENERAL

Small Groups

Two 45-minute class periods

LAB RATINGS LESS ← → MORE

Teacher Prep — 2

Student Setup — 4

Cleanup — 2

MATERIALS

For each group

- hammer
- measuring tape, metric
- paper
- paper fastener, small metal
- pencil
- protractor with a small hole in its base
- push pin
- straw, large plastic
- string, 12 m long
- tape, masking
- wooden stakes, 2

For each student

- safety goggles

SAFETY INFORMATION

Remind students to review all safety cautions and icons before beginning this lab. Caution students to take care when using the hammer.

TEACHER NOTES

In this activity, students construct a sextant from the provided materials and use it to make a map. To do this, each group finds an area that has at least three tall objects, such as a tree, a building, and a flagpole. The objects should be relatively close together (perhaps no more than 10 meters apart). Also, they should probably be in a grassy area so that stakes can be hammered into the ground. If the ground is too hard, or there isn't any grass, students can use cones instead of stakes than they can tie string to the cones. After establishing a baseline, the group uses the sextant to measure the angles between the baseline and the objects. Students also measure distances between pairs of objects using a tape measure. The data are used to construct a scaled map.

Tip This activity will help students understand that tools and instruments can help scientists make observations or measurements that cannot be detected by senses alone.

Skills Focus Making Measurements, Constructing Maps

My Notes

MODIFICATION FOR INDEPENDENT Inquiry

Challenge students to develop a method for using the sextant to measure angles between objects. Then challenge them to use angle information that they acquire to create a map showing the relative locations of the objects.

Field Lab continued

Answer Key for DIRECTED Inquiry

IDENTIFY A PROBLEM

1. Sample answer: If we can measure both the distances and angles between objects, we should be able to make an accurate map to show how these objects are related.
   Teacher prompt Is it enough to simply measure the distance between objects or would you need other information also?

MAKE OBSERVATIONS

5. Accept all reasonable answers. See sample in the first table below.
6. Accept all reasonable answers. See sample in the first table below.
7. Accept all reasonable answers. See sample in the first table below.

ANGLE INFORMATION

Object	Angle from Stake A	Angle from Stake B
Tree	73°	45°
Flagpole	38°	40°
Streetlight	42°	73°

8. Accept all reasonable answers. See sample in the table labeled "Distance Information" below.

DISTANCE INFORMATION

Object 1	Object 2	Actual distance (m)	Map distance (cm)
Tree	Flagpole	4.5	4.5
Tree	Streetlight	5	5
Flagpole	Streetlight	4	4

ANALYZE THE RESULTS

9. Accept all reasonable answers. See sample in the table labeled "Distance Information" above.

Field Lab continued

10. Accept all reasonable answers. Sample map:

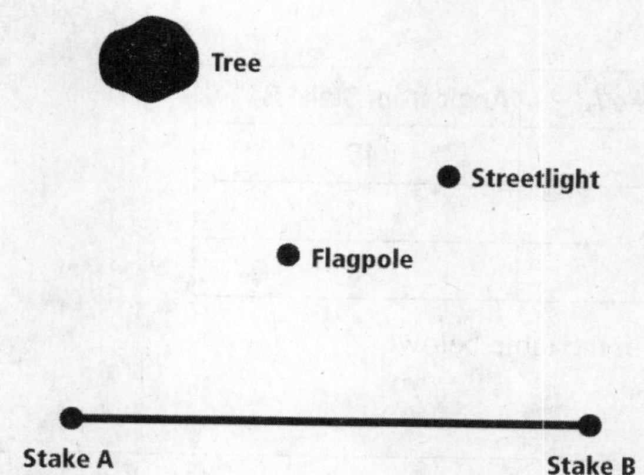

DRAW CONCLUSIONS

11. Sample answer: We used the sextant to measure angles between the objects and the baseline. This allowed us to determine the locations of the objects relative to each other.

Teacher prompt What did you actually measure with the sextant and why?

Connect TO THE ESSENTIAL QUESTION

12. Sample answer: Almost any unit of distance can be used to create a map. Different units would be used at a different scale. For example, a map of the schoolyard might use meters scaled to centimeters as for this lab. But a map of the United States using meters scaled to centimeters would be impractical. For a map of a very large area you want to use large scale units scaled down to small scale units, such as kilometers scaled to millimeters.

Teacher prompt How do we represent a very large area on to an area of paper suitable for a map?

Answer Key for GUIDED Inquiry

IDENTIFY A PROBLEM

1. Sample answer: If we can measure both the distances and angles between objects, we should be able to make an accurate map to show how these objects are related.

Teacher prompt Is it enough to simply measure the distance between objects or would you need other information also?

MAKE OBSERVATIONS

5. Accept all reasonable answers. See sample in the table below.

6. Accept all reasonable answers. See sample in the table below.

Field Lab continued

7. Accept all reasonable answers. See sample in the table below.

ANGLE INFORMATION

Object	Angle from Stake A	Angle from Stake B
Tree	73°	45°
Flagpole	38°	40°
Streetlight	42°	73°

8. Accept all reasonable answers. See sample in the table below.

DISTANCE INFORMATION

Object 1	Object 2	Actual distance (m)	Map distance (cm)
Tree	Flagpole	4.5	4.5
Tree	Streetlight	5	5
Flagpole	Streetlight	4	4

ANALYZE THE RESULTS

9. Sample answer: The mapped area is 10 m × 10 m. If the paper is 20 cm × 15 cm, it will accommodate an area of 10 cm × 10 cm. Therefore a suitable scale is 1 m of actual distance to be equivalent to 1 cm on the map.

10. Accept all reasonable answers. See sample in the table labeled "Distance Information" above.

11. Accept all reasonable answers. Sample map:

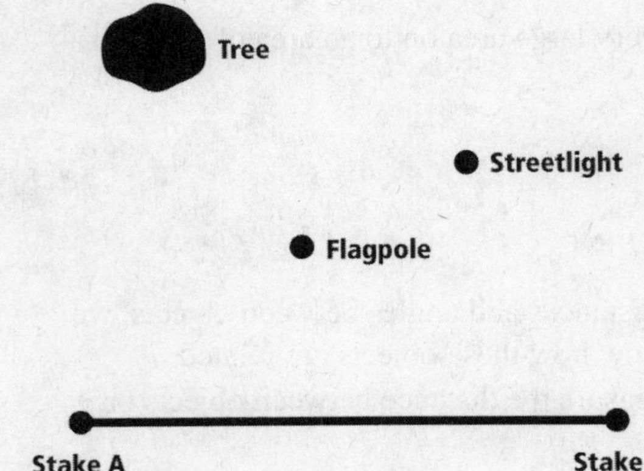

Field Lab continued

DRAW CONCLUSIONS

12. Sample answer: We used the sextant to measure angles between the objects and the baseline. This allowed us to determine the locations of the objects relative to each other.

Teacher prompt What did you actually measure with the sextant and why?

Connect TO THE ESSENTIAL QUESTION

13. Sample answer: Almost any unit of distance can be used to create a map. Different units would be used at a different scale. For example, a map of the schoolyard might use meters scaled to centimeters for this lab. However a map of the United States using meters scaled to centimeters would be impractical. For a map of a very large area you want to use large-scale units scaled down to small-scale units, such as kilometers scaled to millimeters.

Teacher prompt How do we represent a very large area on to an area of paper suitable for a map?

Name ________________ Class ____________ Date ____________

FIELD LAB DIRECTED *Inquiry*

Use a Sextant to Make a Map

In this lab, you will select an outdoor area and then take the measurements you need to make a scaled map of the area. As part of the lab you will make and use an instrument called a sextant to collect some of the data you need to make an accurate map.

OBJECTIVES

- Construct a sextant and use it to make a scaled map of an outdoor area.

MATERIALS

For each group

- hammer
- measuring tape, metric
- paper
- paper fastener, small metal
- pencil
- protractor with a small hole in its base
- push pin
- straw, large plastic
- string, 12 m long
- tape, masking
- wooden stakes, 2

For each student

- safety goggles

PROCEDURE

IDENTIFY A PROBLEM

1. Suppose you want to create a map to show how different objects are located with respect to one another in an outdoor area. What information would you need to collect to be able to make an accurate map of these objects?

   ____

   ____

   ____

2. Build a sextant. Use the push pin to poke a small hole through the center of the straw. Push the ends of the metal paper fastener through the hole. Put the ends of the paper fastener into the hole in the protractor. Spread the metal ends. Make sure the straw can spin freely.

Name ______________________ Class ______________ Date ______________

Field Lab continued

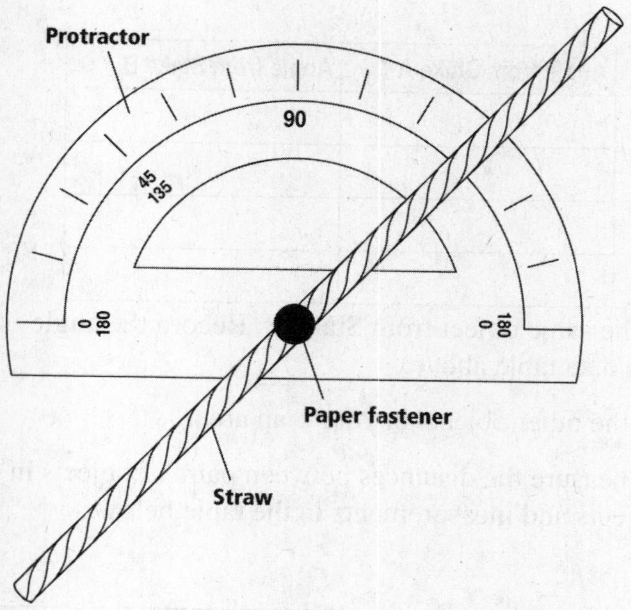

MAKE OBSERVATIONS

3. Take your sextant and the other materials outdoors.

4. Find an area to map. Your area should have at least three large objects, such as a flagpole, a tree, and a building. To prepare the area you will map, use the tape measure to mark off the length and width of the area that includes the three objects. Designate one side as the baseline. Hammer one wooden stake into the ground at one end of the baseline. Hammer the other stake into the ground at the other end of the baseline. Make sure the tops of the stakes are level. Tie a string from one stake to the other. Label the stakes A and B. This string represents the baseline.

5. Use your sextant to measure the angles between the objects and the baseline. Use the masking tape to tape your sextant to Stake A. The base of the protractor should line up with your baseline. Find an object to sight in your map area. Write the name of the object in the data table. Look down the length of the straw to line it up with the object. Keep the straw still. Look at the angle the straw makes on the protractor. Write this angle in the second column of the data table.

ANGLE INFORMATION

Object	Angle from Stake A	Angle from Stake B

6. Repeat Step 5, but sight the same object from Stake B. Record the angle in the third column of the data table above.
7. Repeat Steps 5 and 6 for the other objects in your map area.
8. Use the tape measure to measure the distances between pairs of objects in your area. Record the objects and measurements in the table below.

DISTANCE INFORMATION

Object 1	Object 2	Actual distance (m)	Map distance (cm)

ANALYZE THE RESULTS

9. **Applying Data** In the classroom, use the following scale for making your map: 1 meter (m) of actual distance equals 1 centimeter (cm) on the map. Use this scale to calculate the map distances that correspond with each real distance. Record these numbers in the third column of the table above.

10 **Drawing Maps** Draw a map using your results by following the procedure below.

a. Make the baseline along the bottom of the paper. Mark the ends of the baseline with dots and label these Stake A and Stake B.

b. Put the protractor on the point labeled Stake A and line it up with the baseline. Mark a point at the correct angle for the first object sighted from Stake A. Use the ruler to draw a straight line from Stake A through the mark.

c. Put the protractor on the point labeled Stake B. Mark a point at the correct angle for the first object sighted from Stake B. Use the ruler to draw a straight line from Stake B through the mark. The object is located where this line meets the other line you drew in Step 10a above. Label this point with the name of the object. Erase the lines.

d. Repeat Steps 10a–10c for each of the other objects on your map.

DRAW CONCLUSIONS

11 **Explaining Results** How did the sextant help you create the map of your area? How would your map have been different if you had not had the sextant to gather data?

____

____

____

Connect TO THE ESSENTIAL QUESTION

12 **Applying Concepts** What other units of length or distance might be used to create maps and why?

____

____

____

____

____

____

Name ______________________ Class ______________ Date ______________

FIELD LAB GUIDED *Inquiry*

Use a Sextant to Make a Map

In this lab, you will select an outdoor area and then take the measurements you need to make a scaled map of the area. As part of the lab you will make and use an instrument called a sextant to collect some of the data you need to make an accurate map.

OBJECTIVES

- Construct a sextant and use it to make a scaled map of an outdoor area.

MATERIALS

For each group
- hammer
- measuring tape, metric
- paper
- paper fastener, small metal
- pencil
- protractor with a small hole in its base
- push pin
- straw, large plastic
- string, 12 m long
- tape, masking
- wooden stakes, 2

For each student
- safety goggles

PROCEDURE

IDENTIFY A PROBLEM

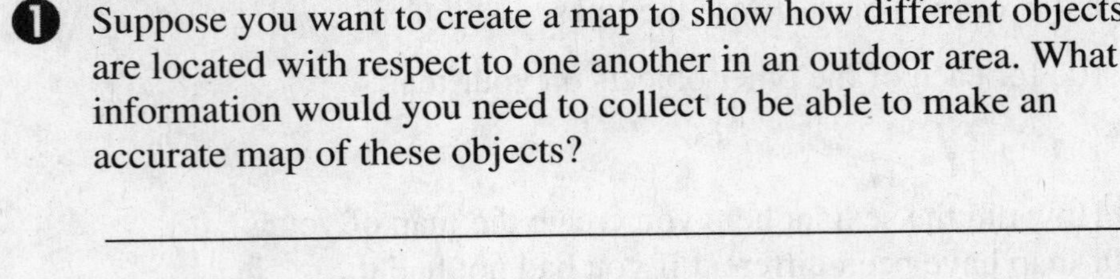

1 Suppose you want to create a map to show how different objects are located with respect to one another in an outdoor area. What information would you need to collect to be able to make an accurate map of these objects?

____

____

____

2 Build a sextant. Use the push pin to poke a small hole through the center of the straw. Push the ends of the metal paper fastener through the hole. Put the ends of the paper fastener into the hole in the protractor. Spread the metal ends. Make sure the straw can spin freely.

Field Lab continued

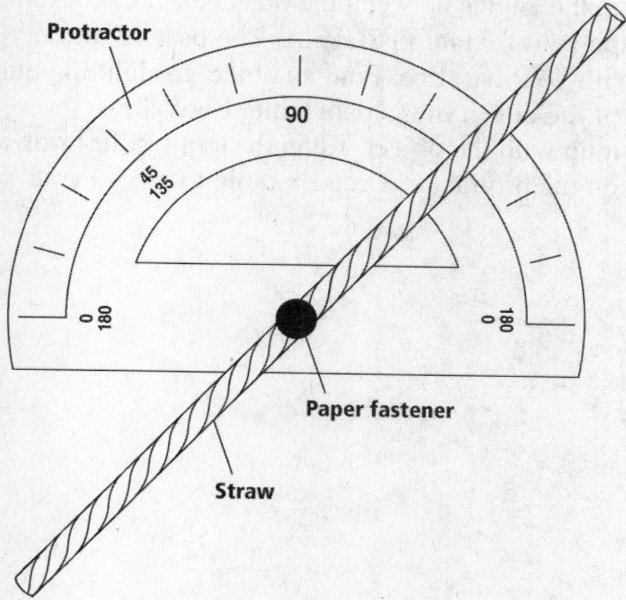

MAKE OBSERVATIONS

3. Take your sextant and the other materials outdoors.

4. Find an area to map. Your area should have at least three large objects, such as a flagpole, a tree, and a building. To prepare the area you will map, use the tape measure to mark off the length and width of the area that includes the three objects. Designate one side as the baseline. Hammer one wooden stake into the ground at one end of the baseline. Hammer the other stake into the ground at the other end of the baseline. Make sure the tops of the stakes are level. Tie a string from one stake to the other.

Field Lab continued

5. Use your sextant to measure the angles between the objects and the baseline. Use the masking tape to tape your sextant to Stake A. The base of the protractor should line up with your baseline. Find an object to sight in your map area. Write the name of the object in the data table. Look down the length of the straw to line it up with the object. Keep the straw still. Look at the angle the straw makes on the protractor. Create a table to record your data.

6. Repeat Step 5, but sight the same object from Stake B. Record the angle in your table.

7. Repeat Steps 5 and 6 for the other objects in your map area.

8. Use the tape measure to measure the distances between pairs of objects in your area. Create a second table to record your data.

Name ______________________ Class ______________ Date ______________

Field Lab continued

ANALYZE THE RESULTS

9 **Applying Data** You need to fit your map on the piece of paper. What would be a suitable scale for your map? Explain why you chose this scale.

____

____

____

10 **Calculating Map Distances** Use the scale you chose to calculate the map distances. Record these numbers in your table.

11 **Drawing Maps** Draw the baseline along the bottom of a separate sheet of paper. Mark the ends of the baseline with dots. Label Stake A and Stake B. Use the protractor, ruler, and pencil to locate the objects on your map based on the data you collected in Steps 5 through 8. Label your map with the object's names.

DRAW CONCLUSIONS

12 **Explaining Results** How did the sextant help you create the map of your area? How would your map have been different if you had not had the sextant to gather data?

____

____

____

Connect TO THE ESSENTIAL QUESTION

13 **Applying Concepts** What other units of length or distance might be used to create maps and why?

____

____

____

____

____

____

QUICK LAB DIRECTED Inquiry

Modeling Eye Images GENERAL

Small groups
15 minutes

MATERIALS

For each group

- fork, plastic
- magnifying lens
- paper, white notebook
- tape, masking (optional)

For each student

- safety goggles

LAB RATINGS

LESS ◄——► MORE

Teacher Prep — 1
Student Setup — 1
Cleanup — 1

SAFETY INFORMATION

Remind students to review all safety cautions and icons before beginning this lab. Caution students to be careful with the plastic forks.

TEACHER NOTES

In this activity, students will model how the lens of the eye projects images onto the retina. A flower, a spoon, or any object with a clear difference between the top and the bottom can be used in place of the fork. They should do the activity in a brightly lit room. Students can tape the paper on which the image will be projected to the wall. If students cannot see the image on the paper, they may need to adjust the position of the lens.

Skills Focus Making Models, Evaluating Models

My Notes

MODIFICATION FOR GUIDED Inquiry

Provide students with the materials. Explain that the lens of the eye forms an image on the back of the eye. Ask students to make a model that shows how images are formed by the eye. Make sure they analyze the image that is formed so that they can explain what they learned from their model.

Answer Key

3. Sample answer: The image is upside down. It looks like a shadow.
4. Sample answer: The model shows that the images that the lens in an eye makes are upside down.
5. Sample answer: It does not show how the eye sees color.
6. Sample answer: Scientists would use a model like this to study how the lens makes images in the eye because they don't need to use a real eye to learn about how images are made.

Name ______________________ Class ______________ Date ______________

QUICK LAB DIRECTED *Inquiry*

Modeling Eye Images

In this lab, you will model how the eye makes images of objects. The lens in the front of the eye makes an image on the back of the eye. You will use a magnifying lens to model how the lens in an eye works.

OBJECTIVE

- Model how the eye makes images.
- Identify the benefits and limitations of models.

MATERIALS

- fork, plastic
- magnifying lens
- paper, white notebook
- tape, masking (optional)

For each student

- safety goggles

PROCEDURE

1. Hold the **magnifying lens** a few centimeters away from the **notebook paper**.
2. Place the **fork** in front of the lens. The lens should be between the fork and the paper.
3. Look for an image of the fork on the paper. Change the distance between the fork and the lens by moving the fork until you see the image. Record your observations.

____

____

____

____

____

____

____

____

____

____

____

____

____

____

Quick Lab continued

4 What does your model demonstrate about the human eye?

5 Describe one thing your model does not show about the eye.

6 Why might a scientist use a model like this one?

QUICK LAB DIRECTED Inquiry

Interpreting Models GENERAL

Student pairs
20–30 minutes

LAB RATINGS LESS ⟷ MORE

Teacher Prep — 1
Student Setup — 1
Cleanup — 1

MATERIALS

For each pair
- paper, blank (1 sheet)
- pencil
- ruler, metric
- scale drawing of human skeleton

My Notes

SAFETY INFORMATION

Remind students to review all safety cautions and icons before beginning this lab.

TEACHER NOTES

In this activity, students will determine the scale of a model, prepare a scale model, and describe the advantages and limitations of models. The scale drawing of the skeleton that you provide should have clearly labeled humerus, tibia, and femur bones. A three-dimensional miniature skeleton could also be used, as long as it is a scale model. Before beginning the activity, you may wish to review the concept of scale and how it relates to models.

Skills Focus Analyzing Data, Evaluating Models, Making Models

MODIFICATION FOR INDEPENDENT Inquiry

Have each student group choose an object or process to model. Objects can be micro, e.g., a plant or animal cell, or macro, e.g., a plan for a city park or farm irrigation system. Examples of processes include circulation of blood and movement of bones around various kinds of joints.

Answer Key

2. Sample answer: humerus, 4.0 cm; femur, 5.0 cm; tibia, 3.6 cm
3. Sample answer: 1 cm = 10 cm, or 1:10
4. for the presentation of data in a limited space; allows for comparison of relative Sample answer: 2 m
5. Advantages: allows sizes of bones. Disadvantages: is not three-dimensional; cannot be manipulated.
6. Sample answer: 1 cm = 20,000 km, or similar, would work well
7. Sample answer: Using a scale of 1 cm = 20,000 km, the diameter of the circles would be Mars, 3.3 mm (0.33 cm); Earth, 6.4 mm (0.64 cm); and Jupiter, 71.4 mm (7.14 cm).

Name ______________________ Class ______________ Date ______________

QUICK LAB DIRECTED Inquiry

Interpreting Models

In this lab, you will determine the scale of a model of a human skeleton. You will describe the advantages and limitations of the model. You will then choose a scale for modeling three planets—Earth, Mars, and Jupiter—so that you can draw circles to represent these planets on a single sheet of paper.

OBJECTIVES

- Determine the scale of a model.
- Make a model to scale.
- Describe the advantages and limitations of models.

MATERIALS

For each pair

- paper, blank (1 sheet)
- pencil
- ruler, metric
- scale drawing of human skeleton

PROCEDURE

1. Examine the **model of the human skeleton** and the data table below.

Bone	Length, actual (cm)	Length, model (cm)
humerus	40	
femur	50	
tibia	36	

2. Measure the lengths of these three bones in the model. Fill in the third column of the table with your data.

3. What is the scale of the model? Show your work.

____

____

____

4. Based on your scale, what is the actual height of the person the model represents? Show your work.

____

____

____

____

Name ______________________ Class ______________ Date ______________

Quick Lab continued

5 Describe the advantages and limitations of the model.

____

____

____

____

____

____

____

____

____

____

____

____

____

6 Earth's diameter is 12,756 km. Mars's diameter is 6,792 km. Jupiter's diameter is 142,984 km. Identify a scale that will allow you to draw circles representing the three planets at their correct relative sizes. Your circles must all fit on a single sheet of paper. What scale should you use?

____

____

____

____

____

____

____

____

____

7 On a separate piece of **paper**, draw and label three circles representing the three planets.

S.T.E.M. LAB DIRECTED Inquiry AND INDEPENDENT Inquiry

Exploring Convection

Student pairs

Two 45-minute class periods

MATERIALS

For each pair
- blocks, wood
- food coloring
- hot plate
- pan, rectangular baking, 7–9 cm high
- paper
- spoon, plastic
- stopwatch
- thermometer
- water

For each student
- gloves, heat-resistant
- lab apron
- safety goggles

My Notes

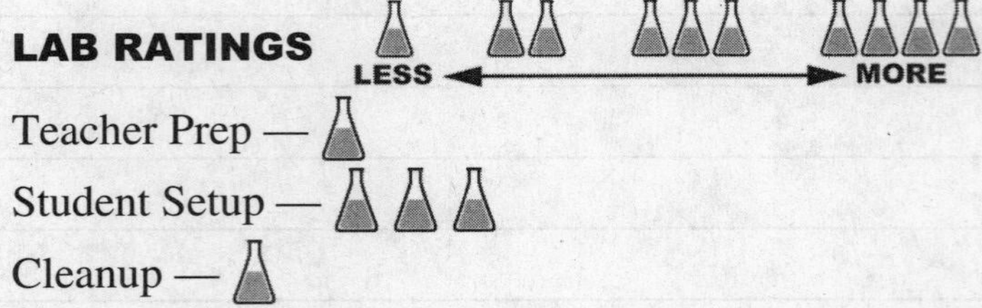

SAFETY INFORMATION

Remind students to review all safety cautions and icons before beginning this lab. Students should not touch the surface of the hot plate. Be sure that students wear heat-resistant gloves when emptying the tray. Have paper towels available to clean up any spills. Spilled water is a slipping hazard and should be cleaned up immediately.

TEACHER NOTES

In this activity, students will build both physical and conceptual models to investigate factors that affect convection. You will want to preview the concept of convection if you have not already covered this material with students.

The surface of the hot plate used should be less than half the length of the baking pan. This will ensure that the heat is applied only to one side of the pan. The pieces of wood that students use should be large enough to separate the baking pan into two sections, allowing only a small amount of water to flow between the sections. You could also use rocks, sheets of aluminum foil, or wax-coated cardboard to divide the container into two sections, with a small gap allowing water to flow between the sections. The goal is to create two separate bodies of water that are only slightly connected, so that only a small amount of water can be exchanged between them. Use a clear glass or Pyrex® baking pan so that students can see what is happening below the water's surface.

You may wish to help students construct tables in which to record their data. Alternatively, you may have them develop their own system for organizing their data.

Tip This activity may help students understand the difference between physical models and conceptual models and the advantages and disadvantages of both.

Skills Focus Building Models, Practicing Lab Techniques

S.T.E.M. Lab continued

MODIFICATION FOR GUIDED Inquiry

Allow students to choose a factor to investigate: initial water temperature, salt content of water, or presence of an obstruction in water. Have students develop a hypothesis and build a physical model to test their hypothesis. They should use the results of the experiment with their physical model and create a conceptual model. Students should present both models to the class and discuss situations in which physical models are more appropriate than conceptual models and vice versa.

Answer Key for DIRECTED Inquiry

ASK A QUESTION

1. Sample answer: A barrier will slow the transfer of heat through the fluid, because it will prevent the fluid from carrying heat. I can show this by making a physical model in which dye moves through heated water containing a barrier. Then I can draw a diagram showing the results of that experiment to make a conceptual model.

BUILD A MODEL

4. Accept all reasonable answers.
6. Accept all reasonable answers.
8. Accept all reasonable answers.
9. Students' drawings should match the results of their physical experiment.

ANALYZE THE RESULTS

10. Sample answer: The presence of a barrier was the independent variable. The amount of water, temperature of water, amount of heat, and location of heat were all controlled.
11. Sample answer: The dye showed the water's path.
12. Sample answer: The physical model used dye to show the movement of water, while the conceptual model used a diagram to explain the concept.
13. Sample answer: The physical model actually showed the process in real time, which made it more effective. The conceptual model was a diagram, but it did not show the process as well as the physical model did.

DRAW CONCLUSIONS

14. Sample answer: A conceptual model would be more likely used to explain convection in the Earth's mantle because you cannot actually see the process.

S.T.E.M. Lab continued

Connect TO THE ESSENTIAL QUESTION

15. Sample answer: Scientists use models and simulations to show how phenomena occur, how systems work, and to predict future events.

Answer Key for INDEPENDENT Inquiry

ASK A QUESTION

1. Sample answer: How does the presence of a barrier affect the movements of convection currents through a fluid? I can make a physical model in which I place a barrier and see how colored water moves across the barrier. I can use the results of that model to draw a conceptual model of the process.

FORM A HYPOTHESIS

2. Sample answer: A barrier will slow the transfer of heat through the fluid, because it will prevent the fluid from flowing and carrying heat.

TEST THE HYPOTHESIS

3. Sample answer: the presence or absence of a barrier

4. Sample answer: amount of water, temperature of water, amount of heat, and location of heat

5. Accept all reasonable procedures.

6. Accept all reasonable answers.

ANALYZE THE RESULTS

7. Sample answer: When there was no barrier, convection currents carried heat from one side of the pan to the other. The temperature of the water on different sides of the pan did not vary much. When there was a barrier, convection currents did not form on the side that was separated from the heat source. The temperature of the water near the heat source was much higher than the water far from the heat source.

8. Sample answer: The physical model used food coloring to show the movement of water, while the conceptual model used diagrams to explain the concept.

9. Sample answer: The physical model actually showed the process in real time, which made it more effective. The conceptual model was a diagram, but it did not show the process as well as the physical model did.

DRAW CONCLUSIONS

10. Sample answer: A conceptual model would be more likely used to explain convection in Earth's mantle because you cannot actually see that process.

Connect TO THE ESSENTIAL QUESTION

11. Answers will vary: Scientists use models and simulations to show how phenomena occur, how systems work, and to predict future events.

Name ______________________ Class ______________ Date ______________

S.T.E.M. LAB DIRECTED Inquiry

Exploring Convection

In this activity, you will build a physical model to show how a barrier affects convection. You will then use your physical model to make a conceptual model. Convection is a form of heat transfer in which the motion of a fluid moves heat from one place to another. Convection is involved in heat transfer in the atmosphere, oceans, and Earth's mantle.

OBJECTIVES

- Build and compare two models of convection.
- Identify and describe factors that affect convection.

MATERIALS

For each pair
- blocks, wood
- food coloring
- hot plate
- pan, rectangular baking, 7–9 cm high
- paper
- spoon, plastic
- stopwatch
- thermometer
- water

For each student
- gloves, heat-resistant
- lab apron
- safety goggles

PROCEDURE

ASK A QUESTION

1. In this lab, you will build a physical model and a conceptual model to answer the following question: How does the presence of a barrier affect convection within a fluid? How can you show this with a physical model? How could you show it with a conceptual model?

BUILD A MODEL

2. Place one end of the pan on the surface of a hot plate. Place the other end on wooden blocks. The container should be level. Fill the container with water to a few centimeters from the top.

3. Drop some food coloring in the pan. Some of the color should stay on the top of the water and some should sink toward the bottom.

4. Use a thermometer to measure the temperature of the water above the hot plate and the water on the opposite side of the pan. Record the temperatures in the table below.

DATA IN ABSENCE OF BARRIER

	Temperature near heat source	Temperature away from heat source
Initial		
2 minutes		
4 minutes		
6 minutes		
8 minutes		
10 minutes		

5. Turn the hot plate to medium and start the stopwatch.

6. Observe the water through the side of the container. Every 2 minutes (min), measure the temperature of the water on both sides of the pan. Record the temperatures in the table. Observe the behavior of the food coloring. What do you see?

____

____

____

____

____

7. After 10 min, turn off the hot plate. One student should wear heat-resistant gloves to carefully lift the pan and empty the water and food coloring into a sink.

8. Repeat Steps 3 to 7, but place wood blocks along the middle of the container to separate the water into two bodies. Only a small amount of water should be able to flow between the two parts of the pan. Make sure you place a drop of food coloring on both sides of the barrier. Record your observations in the table below.

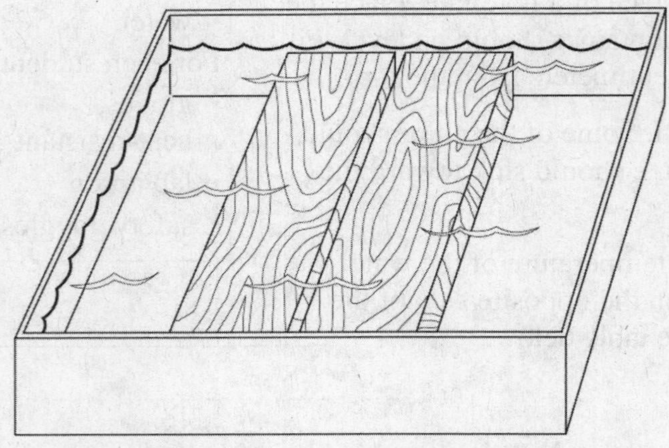

DATA IN PRESENCE OF BARRIER

	Temperature near heat source	Temperature away from heat source
Initial		
2 minutes		
4 minutes		
6 minutes		
8 minutes		
10 minutes		

Name ______________________ Class ______________ Date ________________

S.T.E.M. Lab continued

9. Using your physical models of convection, draw a conceptual model of convection.

ANALYZE THE RESULTS

10. **Analyzing Methods** Consider your physical model. What was the independent variable in this experiment? Which variables were controlled?

11. **Analyzing Methods** What was the purpose of the food coloring in this experiment?

12. **Comparing Results** How does each model show convection differently?

Name ______________________ Class ______________ Date ______________

S.T.E.M. Lab continued

13 **Comparing Methods** Which model do you think was a more effective way to show convection? Explain.

____

____

____

____

____

DRAW CONCLUSIONS

14 **Applying Concepts** Which type of model is most likely to be used to explain convection in the Earth's mantle? Why?

____

____

____

____

Connect TO THE ESSENTIAL QUESTION

15 **Synthesize Information** How do scientists use models and simulations to represent systems, explain phenomena, and make predictions?

____

____

____

Name ______________________ Class ______________ Date ______________

S.T.E.M. LAB INDEPENDENT Inquiry

Exploring Convection

In this activity, you will build a physical model to show how a barrier affects convection. You will then use your physical model to make a conceptual model. Convection is a form of heat transfer in which the motion of a fluid moves heat from one place to another. Convection is involved in heat transfer in the atmosphere, oceans, and Earth's mantle.

OBJECTIVES

- Build and compare two models of convection.
- Identify and describe factors that affect convection.

MATERIALS

For each pair
- blocks, wood
- food coloring
- hot plate
- pan, rectangular baking, 7–9 cm high
- paper
- spoon, plastic
- stopwatch
- thermometer
- water

For each student
- gloves, heat-resistant
- lab apron
- safety goggles

PROCEDURE

ASK A QUESTION

1. Identify a testable question about factors that affect convection. How can you show this with a physical model and a conceptual one?

____

____

____

____

FORM A HYPOTHESIS

2. Write a hypothesis for your question. Remember that a hypothesis must include a prediction about what you will observe and an explanation for why you made that prediction.

____

____

____

____

____

____

____

TEST THE HYPOTHESIS

3. What will be the independent variable in a physical model of your experiment?

____

____

4 What variables will you control in your experiment?

____

____

5 On a separate sheet of paper, describe the procedure you will use to build a physical model to test your hypothesis. Identify the data you will collect, and explain how you will collect and organize the data. Include a list of the materials you will need. Then explain how you will use the physical model to make a conceptual model of convection.

6 Show your plan to your teacher. When your teacher has approved your procedure, carry it out. Record your results on your paper.

ANALYZE THE RESULTS

7 **Describing Results** What were the results of your experiment?

____

____

____

____

____

____

8 **Comparing Results** How did each model show convection differently?

____

____

____

____

S.T.E.M. Lab continued

9 **Comparing Methods** Which model do you think was a more effective way to show convection? Explain.

____

____

____

____

____

DRAW CONCLUSIONS

10 **Applying Concepts** Which type of model is most likely to be used to explain convection in Earth's mantle? Why?

____

____

____

____

Connect TO THE ESSENTIAL QUESTION

11 **Synthesize Information** How do scientists use models and simulations to represent systems, explain phenomena, and make predictions?

____

____

____

QUICK LAB INDEPENDENT *Inquiry*

Designing a Consumer Product BASIC

Small groups
30 minutes

MATERIALS
For each group
- markers
- paper
- poster board or construction paper

LAB RATINGS

LESS ⟷ MORE

Teacher Prep — 1 flask
Student Setup — 1 flask
Cleanup — 1 flask

My Notes

TEACHER NOTES

In this activity, students will work in small groups to develop a design concept for a new consumer product. Provide students with the following scenario: a venture capital firm is seeking to fund the manufacture of an innovative product. Students are to brainstorm ideas for a design proposal.

As preparation for the activity, have the students decide—as a class—what kind of product they would like to design. All groups will work on the same product type. For homework, have each student come up with a basic idea that addresses the design challenge. The ideas do not have to be well developed, and students should be cautioned against being too invested in their ideas at the beginning of the activity because the class will select only one product for the groups to design.

Have each group use their pooled ideas to jumpstart a short brainstorming session for proposed solutions to the design challenge. Instruct each group to select one concept and draw a picture of its product concept on poster board. The designs should use currently available technology. Tell the students that their drawings should include a title, a short list of features, labels for all materials used, and an estimated total materials cost for the final product. (For this activity there are no stated limits on the design, including cost.)

Have each group hold up its poster and give a 1-minute (min) description of its product idea. As a setup for the next lab, guide a brief, deliberately (and perhaps humorously) haphazard discussion of the merits and/or disadvantages of the alternatives, and allow the students to vote for the choice they "like best." Collect and retain the product design concepts for use in the next lab.

Suggested Pacing Introduction and planning, 15–20 min; descriptions, 5–10 min; discussions and voting, 5 min.

Tip Although selecting from among potential solutions is one of the essential steps in the engineering design process, it is not always done formally. This activity allows students to experience an informal process, which will be compared with a more organized approach in the next lab.

Skills Focus Developing Creative Solutions, Participating in Working Groups

Quick Lab continued

MODIFICATION FOR GUIDED *Inquiry*

Instead of a class discussion to come up with a product on which to work, present the class with a short list of possible products on which they can vote, or select one topic for them. Ideas for possible products include a water toy for a blind child, a playground for a middle school, and a musical instrument.

Answer Key

1. The answer provided should match the class choice.
2. Accept all reasonable answers.
4. Accept all reasonable answers.
7. Answers may vary but should be supported with reasons.
8. The answer provided should match the class choice.
9. List: Identify a need, conduct research, brainstorm solutions, select a solution, build a prototype, test and evaluate the prototype, redesign to improve, and communicate the results. ("Brainstorm solutions" and "select a solution" should be circled.)

Name ______________________ Class ____________ Date ________________

QUICK LAB INDEPENDENT *Inquiry*

Designing a Consumer Product

An essential step in the engineering design process is brainstorming possible solutions to fill an identified need. Imagine that a venture capital firm is seeking to fund the manufacturing of an innovative product, and that your group is preparing to submit a design proposal for consideration.

OBJECTIVE

- Brainstorm and select from among creative ideas for a new product.

MATERIALS

For each group

- markers
- paper
- poster board or construction paper

PROCEDURE

1. Work as a class to develop concepts for the product. Record the product to be designed.

   ____

2. Work with your group to collect ideas each member has already thought of for the product. Record brief descriptions of the starting ideas below. Remember that the designs must use only currently available technology and materials.

   ____

   ____

   ____

3. Work with your group to develop the ideas in a short brainstorming session. Write out ideas and sketches on paper to help communicate ideas to other members of your group.

4. Work with your group to select a single concept to present to the class. This concept may be based on one, or a combination, of the starting ideas, or may consist of a new idea that your group came up with during the brainstorming session. Record a short description of the idea that your group decides to present.

   ____

   ____

5. Working with your group, draw a picture of your product design with the markers and the poster board. Be detailed. Label your drawing with a creative name for the product and provide a list of features, a list of materials used, and an estimate of the total materials cost of your product.

6. When your group has finished the drawing, present it to the class with a brief description.

Name ______________________ Class ______________ Date ______________

Quick Lab continued

7. Of all the groups' design concepts, which do you think is the best and why?

8. As a class, discuss the different design concepts and vote for the best concept. Record the name of the product design that was selected by the class vote.

9. List the steps of the engineering design process. Circle the steps that you performed in this activity.

QUICK LAB GUIDED Inquiry

Technology, Engineering, and Science GENERAL

Student pairs
20 minutes

LAB RATINGS LESS ← → MORE

Teacher Prep —
Student Setup —
Cleanup —

MATERIALS

For each pair
- artificial animal fur
- cockle-bur
- hook-and-loop fastener (Velcro®)
- magnifying lens

My Notes

TEACHER NOTES

In this activity, students work in pairs to examine the construction of the fruit of a cockle-bur (*Xanthium*) and then guess which type of clothing fastener may have been inspired by the bur structure. Students will be asked to write three sentences that explain the relationship between science, engineering, and technology in terms of burs and hook-and-loop fasteners.

Tip Students will be most successful at writing their summary sentences if they have encountered the terms *science*, *engineering*, and *technology* before undertaking this activity.

Skills Focus Comparing Structures, Recognizing Patterns

MODIFICATION FOR DIRECTED Inquiry

Provide student pairs with a sample of a hook-and-loop fastener at the outset of the activity so that they are not asked to guess which type of fastener was invented.

Answer Key

3. Sample answer: The little hooks sticking out from the fruit would allow it to hang on to fur or cloth.
4. Sample answer: The seed could be carried far from where the plant is located. This would allow the plant to start growing in many other areas on Earth.
5. Answers will vary. Students should eventually identify Velcro® as the fastener that was inspired by the cockle-bur.

Quick Lab continued

7. Accept all reasonable answers. Students should observe that there are two different surfaces to a hook-and-loop fastener. One side has hooks that are similar to the bur structure. The other side has loops that are similar to animal fur or human clothing.

8. Sample answer: Science was used to study the structure of the bur. An engineer used this information to design and make hook-and-loop fasteners. These fasteners are a technology that resulted from applying scientific knowledge to the field of engineering. **Teacher Prompt** Which was involved first in the story of this invention—science, engineering, or technology?

Name ______________________ Class ______________ Date ______________

QUICK LAB GUIDED *Inquiry*

Technology, Engineering, and Science

Throughout history, humans have developed many ways to make their lives easier. Many labor-saving devices were invented by people who thought carefully about how to apply knowledge to meet human needs. In this activity, you will follow this same thinking process as you investigate how burs inspired an inventor to design a clothing fastener. Then you will summarize how this example relates to science, engineering, and technology.

OBJECTIVE

- Investigate burs and how they inspired an idea for a clothing fastener. Use this experience in explaining the differences between technology, engineering, and science.

MATERIALS

For each pair

- artificial animal fur
- cockle-bur
- hook-and-loop fastener (Velcro®)
- magnifying lens

PROCEDURE

1. With your partner, study the image below. It shows a bur, which is a type of fruit produced by some plants. Inside of this structure is a seed.

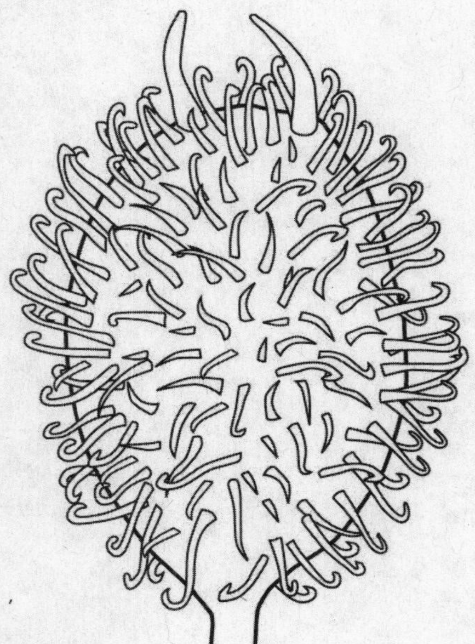

2. Obtain a cockle-bur and square of artificial animal fur from your teacher. Take turns examining how the bur sticks to the animal's fur.

3. What structure of the cockle-bur allows the bur to attach to an animal's fur? Explain.

____

____

4. Why would the bur's ability to cling to animal fur or to human clothing be an advantage for the plant?

____

____

Quick Lab continued

5. Now work with your partner to write down five or six different fasteners that have been invented to secure clothing and shoes. A zipper is one example to get you started. Write your list of fasteners below. Next to each, write "yes" or "no" to indicate whether or not the structure of a cockle-bur might have been an inspiration for its invention.

____

____

____

____

6. Repeat Step 5 until you have at least one type of fastener listed that you think could have been inspired by the bur structure.

7. Obtain a sample from your teacher of the fastener that was inspired by the bur structure. Examine the structure of the fastener with a magnifying lens. Explain what structural features of the fastener are similar to the bur and why that could be applied to making a clothing fastener. Draw a diagram to illustrate.

8. With your partner, discuss the differences between science, engineering, and technology. Use your experience with the bur-inspired clothing fastener as a basis for your discussion. Then write three sentences below that relate science, engineering, and technology to the development of the clothing fastener inspired by burs.

____

____

____

____

____

____

____

____

S.T.E.M. LAB GUIDED *Inquiry* AND INDEPENDENT *Inquiry*

Earthquake Engineering Design Challenge GENERAL

Small groups
45 minutes

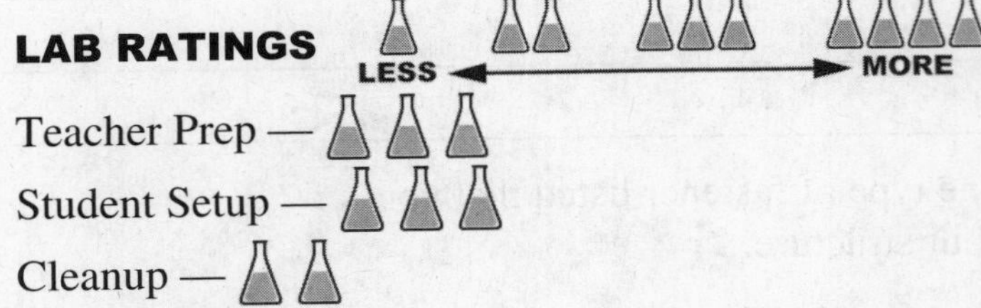

LAB RATINGS

LESS ⟷ MORE

Teacher Prep — 3
Student Setup — 3
Cleanup — 2

SAFETY INFORMATION

Remind students to review all safety cautions and icons before beginning this lab. Tell students they should be cautious when using the shake table so that the marbles remain in the box lid. Any marbles that spill out should be collected immediately. In addition, inform students to exercise care around others when using scissors or other sharp tools. Have students wear safety goggles when using the shake table to avoid any harm from a piece flying off a structure that collapses.

TEACHER NOTES

Build the shake table(s) in advance. You will need at least one shake table for the class; one per group is recommended. To make a shake table, cut a flat piece of cardboard so that it fits inside a large box lid. The flat cardboard should be 4 centimeters (cm) smaller than the lid on all sides. Staple a rubber band to each corner of the flat piece of cardboard. Place marbles inside the box lid. Set the flat piece of cardboard on top of the marbles. Make a hole in each corner of the box lid and pull one rubber band through each hole. Staple the ends of the rubber bands to the box lid so that the bands are somewhat stretched. The inner cardboard piece should shake when pulled to one side and then released. A completed shake table is shown as follows:

MATERIALS

For the shake table
- box lids, large (2)
- marbles (40)
- rubber bands (4)
- stapler

For each group (directed inquiry)
- cardboard, 15 cm × 15 cm
- clay, modeling
- paper
- ruler, metric
- scissors
- stirring sticks, wooden (30)
- stopwatch (or clock with second hand)

For each group (independent inquiry)
- cardboard, 15 cm × 15 cm
- cardboard tubes
- clay, modeling
- craft sticks
- paper
- paper clips
- rubber bands
- ruler, metric
- scissors
- stirring sticks, wooden
- string
- stopwatch (or clock with second hand)
- tape

For each student
- safety goggles

S.T.E.M. Lab continued

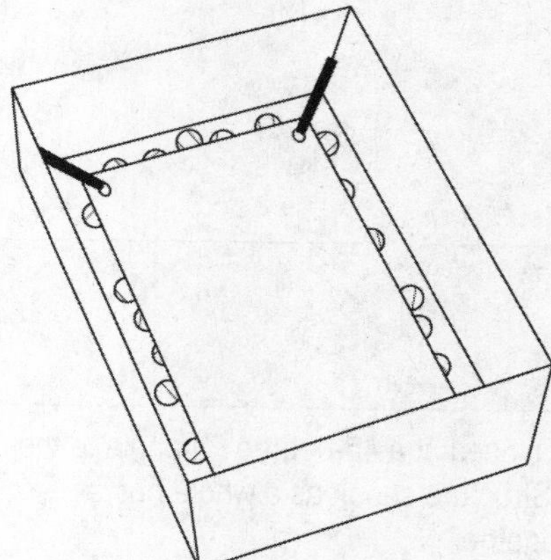

The research component of the engineering design process can be done as homework in advance of the activity.

Tip This activity will help students experience all the steps in the engineering design process.

Skills Focus Building a Model, Drawing Conclusions, Communicating Results

MODIFICATION FOR DIRECTED *Inquiry*

Direct students to build and test two structures: an open box tower and a structure with diagonal bracing.

Answer Key for GUIDED *Inquiry*

RESEARCH A PROBLEM

1. Answers will vary.

DEVELOP A PLAN

2. Answers will vary. Accept all reasonable designs.
3. Answers will vary. Sample answer: Our structure will be made of cubes stacked on cubes. Each cube will have diagonal braces for added support.
   Teacher Prompt How will you decide which design will be the best solution?

FORM A HYPOTHESIS

4. Answers will vary. Sample answer: If a structure is built to include diagonal braces, then when an earthquake causes the ground to shake, the structure will not wobble and fall down because the diagonal braces hold the sides in place.

S.T.E.M. Lab continued

TEST THE HYPOTHESIS

8. Answers will vary. Sample answers:

SHAKE TABLE TEST DATA

Trial number	Distance platform pulled to side (cm)	Notes
1	2	Structure placed at a 45-degree (°) angle to the shaking. Structure shook as a whole but is holding together.
2	2	Top two-thirds of structure is loosening.
3	2	One vertical post and one diagonal brace have come loose.
4	2	Structure collapsed.

ANALYZE RESULTS

9. Answers will vary. Sample answer: The structure was damaged starting with the second trial. After that, every trial made it worse until it collapsed on the fourth trial.

10. Answers will vary. Sample answer: The connections near the bottom weakened first. Sides without diagonal bracing failed before those with bracing.

DRAW CONCLUSIONS

11. Answers will vary. Sample answer: The diagonal braces did seem to help strengthen the structure, but our isolating base didn't move well in the direction of the shaking, so it didn't look like it helped.

12. Answers will vary. Sample answer: For testing next time, we could just shake the table continuously and time how long it takes the structure to fall down.
Teacher Prompt Can you think of another way to use the shake table?

Connect TO THE ESSENTIAL QUESTION

13. Sample answer: The information lets me know what types of structures do and don't work so I can improve my next design.

Answer Key for INDEPENDENT Inquiry

RESEARCH A PROBLEM

1. Answers will vary.

DEVELOP A PLAN

2. Answers will vary. Accept all reasonable designs.

S.T.E.M. Lab continued

3. Answers will vary. Sample answer: Our structure will be made of a paper towel tube core with walls made of craft sticks held together with strips of duct tape. Pieces of string will make diagonal braces on every side.
Teacher Prompt How will you decide which design will be the best solution?

FORM A HYPOTHESIS

4. Answers will vary. Sample answer: If a structure is built to include diagonal braces, then when an earthquake causes the ground to shake, the structure will not wobble and fall down because the diagonal braces hold the sides in place.

TEST THE HYPOTHESIS

7. Answers will vary. Sample answers:

SHAKE TABLE TEST DATA

Trial number	Distance platform pulled to side (cm)	Notes
1	2	Structure placed at a 45-degree (°) angle to the shaking. Structure shook as a whole but is holding together.
2	2	Top two-thirds of structure is loosening.
3	2	One vertical post and one diagonal brace have come loose.
4	2	Structure collapsed.

ANALYZE RESULTS

9. Answers will vary. Sample answer: The structure was damaged starting with the second trial. After that, every trial made it worse until it collapsed during the fourth trial.
10. Answers will vary. Sample answer: The connections near the bottom weakened first. Sides without diagonal bracing failed before those with bracing.

DRAW CONCLUSIONS

11. Answers will vary. Sample answer: The diagonal braces did seem to help strengthen the structure, but our isolating base didn't move well in the direction of the shaking, so it didn't look like it helped.
12. Answers will vary. Sample answer: For testing next time, we could just shake the table continuously and time how long it takes the structure to fall down.
Teacher Prompt Can you think of another way to use the shake table?

Connect TO THE ESSENTIAL QUESTION

13. Sample answer: The information lets me know what types of structures do and don't work, so I can improve my next design.

Name ______________________ Class ______________ Date ______________

S.T.E.M. LAB GUIDED *Inquiry*

Earthquake Engineering Design Challenge

In many areas of the world, earthquakes threaten structures used by humans. Engineers are interested in finding ways to build structures that can safely withstand earthquakes and are constantly developing innovative solutions to the problem. In this activity, you will work with your group to design, build, and test a structure for its ability to resist a simulated earthquake.

OBJECTIVES

- Use the engineering design process.
- Build a 30-centimeter (cm) structure on a 15 cm × 15 cm-square piece of cardboard.
- Test the structure for its resistance to a simulated earthquake.

MATERIALS

For the class:

- shake table

For each group:

- cardboard, 15 cm × 15 cm
- clay, modeling
- paper
- ruler, metric
- scissors
- stirring sticks, wooden (30)
- stopwatch (or clock with second hand)

For each student

- safety goggles

PROCEDURE

RESEARCH A PROBLEM

1. Research earthquake-resistant structure design to learn more about it. What interesting ideas did you find?

____

____

____

DEVELOP A PLAN

2. Work with your group to discuss design features that may help a structure withstand an earthquake. Brainstorm ideas for your structure that have these features. Use paper to communicate your ideas with your group. As a group, draw sketches of three ideas on the planning chart.

PLANNING CHART: SHAKE-RESISTANT STRUCTURES

Design 1	Design 2	Design 3

❸ Compare your three designs and decide on the design that you predict will best withstand earthquakes. Describe your final design proposal below and have your teacher check it before proceeding.

____

____

____

____

FORM A HYPOTHESIS

❹ Use the features you included in your final design proposal to complete the following hypothesis sentence:

If a structure is built to include ______________________, then when an earthquake causes the ground to shake, the structure will ________________ because ____.

BUILD A MODEL

❺ Work with your group to gather materials and build your selected structure using the 15 cm × 15 cm piece of cardboard as a base. Use scissors to cut stirring sticks if you need smaller pieces.

❻ Draw a diagram of the completed structure in the space below.

❼ Lift the structure by the cardboard base and place it on the shake table.

TEST THE HYPOTHESIS

❽ Pull the shake table platform about 2 cm to one side. Release it. Observe how the structure reacts and use Table 2 to record your data. Repeat trials until the structure begins to collapse. Be careful to pull and release the shake table the same way each time.

Name ______________________ Class ______________ Date ______________

S.T.E.M. Lab continued

SHAKE TABLE TEST DATA

Trial number	Distance platform pulled to side (cm)	Notes

ANALYZE RESULTS

9 **Examining Data** What happened to your structure?

____

____

10 **Analyzing Observations** Describe possible weak areas of the structure.

____

____

DRAW CONCLUSIONS

11 **Evaluating Hypotheses** After analyzing your data, is your hypothesis supported? Discuss why or why not.

____

____

12 **Evaluating Methods** Did the testing method challenge your structure? What changes to the testing procedure would you make for the future?

____

____

Connect TO THE ESSENTIAL QUESTION

13 **Evaluating Data** How would the information gathered from this lab be useful if you were to continue to design earthquake-resistant structures beyond this lab experience?

____

____

____

Name ______________________ Class ______________ Date ______________

S.T.E.M. LAB INDEPENDENT *Inquiry*

Earthquake Engineering Design Challenge

In many areas of the world, earthquakes threaten structures used by humans. Engineers are interested in finding ways to build structures that can safely withstand earthquakes and are constantly developing innovative solutions to the problem. In this activity, you will work with your group to design, build, and test a structure for its ability to resist a simulated earthquake.

OBJECTIVES

- Use the engineering design process.
- Build a 30-centimeter (cm) structure on a 15 cm × 15 cm-square piece of cardboard.
- Test the structure for its resistance to a simulated earthquake.

MATERIALS

For the class:

- shake table

For each group:

- cardboard, 15 cm × 15 cm
- cardboard tubes
- clay, modeling
- craft sticks
- paper
- paper clips
- rubber bands
- ruler, metric
- scissors
- stirring sticks, wooden
- string
- stopwatch (or clock with second hand)
- tape

For each student

- safety goggles

PROCEDURE

RESEARCH A PROBLEM

1 Research earthquake-resistant structure design to learn more about it. What interesting ideas did you find?

____

____

____

DEVELOP A PLAN

2 Work with your group to discuss design features that may help a structure withstand an earthquake. Brainstorm ideas for your structure that have these features. Use paper to communicate your ideas with your group. As a group, draw sketches of three ideas on the planning chart.

PLANNING CHART: SHAKE-RESISTANT STRUCTURES

Design 1	Design 2	Design 3

3 Compare your three designs and decide on the design that you predict will best withstand earthquakes. Describe your final design proposal below and have your teacher check it before proceeding.

____

____

____

____

FORM A HYPOTHESIS

4 Use the features you included in your final design proposal to complete the following hypothesis sentence:

If a structure is built to include _______________, then when an earthquake causes the ground to shake, the structure will _______________ because _______________.

BUILD A MODEL

5 Work with your group to gather materials and build your selected structure using the 15 cm × 15 cm piece of cardboard as a base.

6 Draw a diagram of the completed structure in the space below.

TEST THE HYPOTHESIS

7 Discuss with your group how you plan to test your structure. Develop a testing plan that includes repeated trials of equivalent steps using the shake table. On the next page, prepare a data table that outlines your testing plan. The table should show what action you will take for each trial and what you plan to observe. Have your teacher approve your plan before you start testing.

8 Conduct tests and record data.

ANALYZE RESULTS

9 **Examining Data** What happened to your structure?

____

____

10 **Analyzing Observations** Describe possible weak areas of the structure.

____

____

DRAW CONCLUSIONS

11 **Evaluating Hypotheses** After analyzing your data, is your hypothesis supported? Discuss why or why not.

____

____

12 **Evaluating Methods** Did the testing method challenge your structure? What changes to the testing procedure would you make for the future?

____

____

Connect TO THE ESSENTIAL QUESTION

13 **Evaluating Data** How would the information gathered from this lab be useful if you were to continue to design earthquake-resistant structures beyond this lab experience?

____

____

____

QUICK LAB GUIDED Inquiry

Investigate Mining BASIC

Small groups
30 minutes

LAB RATINGS

LESS ⟷ MORE

Teacher Prep — 2
Student Setup — 1
Cleanup — 2

SAFETY INFORMATION

Remind students to review all safety cautions and icons before beginning this lab. Caution students to pick up any spilled beads as these could cause slipping.

TEACHER NOTES

In this activity, students will carry out simulated mining activities and observe the effects of factors such as abundance, mining technology, and environmental impact on business operations. You can cut off the top portion of a gallon plastic milk container for students to use to hold the sand, beads, birdseed, and sunflower seeds.

Tip Emphasize that, just as in real life, the price of a resource or commodity does not necessarily include all of the costs associated with the extraction or production of it. Mesh sink strainers can be purchased easily at most stores that sell plumbing products. A cooking strainer can also be used.

Student Tip Think in terms of all your resources, including equipment, time, money, and environmental state. It isn't just about the money!

Skills Focus Analyzing Results

MODIFICATION FOR INDEPENDENT Inquiry

Divide students into teams and give each team a fixed amount of money to start with. For an added challenge, restrict the availability of certain technologies or information.

MATERIALS

For each group

- beads, small red (2)
- beads, medium blue (4)
- beaker, large
- birdseed mix with sunflower seeds (1 lb)
- plastic container
- piece of wire screening
- sand
- stopwatch or clock with second hand

For each student

- safety goggles

My Notes

Quick Lab continued

Answer Key for GUIDED Inquiry

3. Accept all reasonable answers.
4. Sample answer: The smaller, rarer beads were hardest to find. The most valuable ores are usually the hardest to find, too.
5. Accept all reasonable answers.
6. Sample answer: Answers will vary depending on what students find and how many times they dig. They should recognize that paying the environmental cost reduces their profit and makes some items not worth digging for.
7. Accept all reasonable answers.
8. Accept all reasonable answers.
9. Sample answer: The technology would have to cost a lot. This is because the technology makes the process so efficient. We could mine a lot faster with the colander or sifter than without, so we could make a lot more money in less time with it.
10. Sample answer: The red beads probably represent gold because they bring in the most money. The blue beads are silver. The sunflower seeds are copper because they bring the least amount of money.

Name ______________________ Class ______________ Date ______________

QUICK LAB GUIDED *Inquiry*

Investigate Mining

In this lab, you will explore some of the benefits and costs associated with mining.

OBJECTIVE

- Investigate the costs and benefits associated with mining.

MATERIALS

For each group

- beads, small red (2)
- beads, medium blue (4)
- beaker, large
- birdseed mix with sunflower seeds (1 lb)
- plastic container
- piece of wire screening
- sand
- stopwatch or clock with second hand

For each student

- safety goggles

PROCEDURE

1. Pour sand into the container until it is nearly full. Add the birdseed and beads to the sand and mix well.

2. Search through the sand and remove the valuable items: seeds, sunflower seeds, and beads. Place each item in a different pile. Take no more than two minutes to do your sorting. Try to disturb the sand as little as possible while you search.

3. Assign the following values to each of the valued items: small seeds \$1, sunflower seeds \$2, blue beads \$3, and red beads \$5. Make a table in the space below to show the numbers of each item you mined and the amount of money you made from that item.

4. How does the difficulty of finding the red beads relate to the difficulty of finding the most valuable ores?

____

____

5. Replace all of the items in the original bowl. Repeat Step 2 with an environmental cost added. Each time you search the pile, subtract \$2 for the environmental cost from your total. Make a table in the space below to show the numbers of each item you mined and the amount of money you made from that item.

❻ Compare your results from the two mining operations you carried out. How does having to pay for environmental costs affect your final total?

❼ Write a hypothesis to explain how the introduction of an advanced mining technology (a small mesh strainer) will affect your performance in the exercise. Be sure your hypothesis includes the word "because."

❽ Repeat Step 2 using the wire screen as a strainer. Use the beaker to collect the sand that passes through the screen. Record your results in a new table.

❾ Technology involves a cost factor. Then why is technology used in processes such as mining?

❿ If the small seeds, sunflower seeds, and beads represent minerals that contain copper, gold, and silver. Which bead or seed is most likely to represent which mineral? Explain your reasoning.

QUICK LAB INDEPENDENT Inquiry

Air Innovation BASIC

Small groups
45 minutes

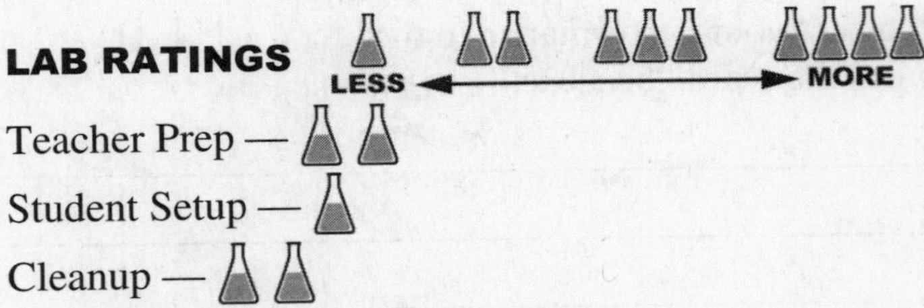

MATERIALS

For each group
- measuring tape
- paper
- paper airplane instructions (optional)
- tape, masking
- toy glider kits (5)
- stopwatch

For each student
- safety goggles

SAFETY INFORMATION

Remind students to review all safety cautions and icons before beginning this lab. Caution students not to aim gliders or planes at other students.

TEACHER NOTES

In this activity, teams of students will optimize a fleet of toy gliders and/or paper airplanes in order to achieve the lowest operational cost. To prepare for the activity, construct a flight corridor for each group on the floor in a classroom or hallway using masking tape to mark off the boundaries. The dimensions of each flight corridor should be 10 meters long by 2 meters wide. To save time, if possible, each group should have their own flight corridor. If necessary, students can use a single glider per group and keep modifying it.

Tip Emphasize with students the importance of evaluating risks and benefits in a systematic manner during this activity. The best technical design may not be feasible for a company operating under safety or financial constraints.

Student Tip Don't get distracted by the looks of the planes. Focus on determining the capability of your planes, then choosing the best design for the job! Or consider appearance as one of the trade offs. What technical advantage would you have to give up for a more attractive appearance?

Skills Focus Making Predictions, Evaluating Alternatives

My Notes

Quick Lab continued

MODIFICATION FOR GUIDED Inquiry

Divide students into teams and give each team access to toy glider kits and materials to construct paper airplanes. Instruct them to build five gliders and five identical paper airplanes. Inform them that they have two minutes to launch their five toy gliders and five paper airplanes. Teams gain 100 points for each plane that crosses the goal line within the flight corridor, 100 points for the plane that flies the farthest past the goal line while still in the flight corridor, and 100 bonus points for the plane that crosses the goal line the fastest. Teams will earn 50 points for each plane that lands within the flight corridor (a rectangle outlined on the floor in masking tape), and subtract 50 points for each plane that flies outside of the corridor to the left or right. One member of the group will time each flight to determine aircraft speed. Teams are allowed to make one modification after each plane test flight.

Answer Key

1. Sample answer: the toy glider is easy to assemble, has uniform construction, and has stiff parts, but can't be modified to make improvements. The paper airplane is inexpensive, easily customizable, and easily tuned but more difficult to make in a consistent manner.
2. Students' tables should have a row for each plane and a column for type, description, flight path results, distance, and speed.
5. Accept all reasonable answers. Students should recognize that when modifications are relatively inexpensive, it pays to make several prototypes. But if modifications are costly, it might make more sense to stick with a slower model that flies reliably than to make expensive modifications while trying to improve speed or distance.
6. Accept all reasonable answers. Students should fill out their tables based on their experiences and they should indicate which plane had the overall best score.

SAMPLE TABLE

Alternatives	Toy Glider	Paper Plane
Quality	++	-
Cost	-	+++
Accuracy	++	+
Ease of assembly	++	-

Name ______________________ Class ______________ Date ______________

QUICK LAB INDEPENDENT *Inquiry*

Air Innovation

In this lab, you will weigh the risks and benefits of using different technologies to make airplanes. To do the analysis, your group will compare the performance of two different types of planes. You will construct and launch five toy gliders and five paper airplanes. You will earn 100 points for each plane that crosses the goal line. You can earn a bonus of 100 points for the plane that travels the farthest past the goal line without going outside the flight corridor to the left or right. You will earn another 100 bonus points for the plane that crosses the goal line the fastest. Fifty points are earned for any plane that lands within the flight corridor and fifty points are lost for every plane that lands outside the corridor to the left or right.

OBJECTIVE

- Investigate the risks and benefits of different technologies as well as modifications to those technologies.

MATERIALS

For each group
- measuring tape
- paper
- paper airplane instructions (optional)
- tape, masking
- toy glider kits (5)
- stopwatch

For each student
- safety goggles

PROCEDURE

1. Within your group, examine the toy glider kits. Discuss the differences between paper airplanes and toy gliders. What are the advantages and disadvantages of each?

   ____

   ____

   ____

   ____

2. Choose a strategy for using paper airplanes and toy gliders that your team believes is best capable of reaching the goal line the highest number of times. Keep in mind the bonus points for distance and speed, and points awarded or lost for being in certain zones when the plane lands. Make a table to record your choices and the results of your test flights below and then construct your planes.

3. Start your test flights. You have two minutes to launch all ten planes. One member of the team will operate the stop watch for each flight. The speed of the flight will only be recorded for planes that reach or pass the goal line. For each of these planes, have another team member measure the total distance the plane flies. After each launch, you can make one modification to the next plane in line.

Name ______________________ Class ____________ Date ______________

Quick Lab continued

4. For each test flight, record the plane type, general description, flight path results, distance, and speed (if applicable).

5. Imagine that you had to pay ten points for each modification to an airplane. Is it worth it? Explain your answer. Would it still be worth it if you had to pay 50 points to modify a plane?

____

____

____

____

____

____

6. Create a table using your experiences with your planes. Select several characteristics to compare between the two planes, then rate each plane with a + or - on each characteristic. Based on your analysis, which plane has the most advantages?

QUICK LAB GUIDED *Inquiry*

Model a Home Heating System GENERAL

Large groups
15 minutes

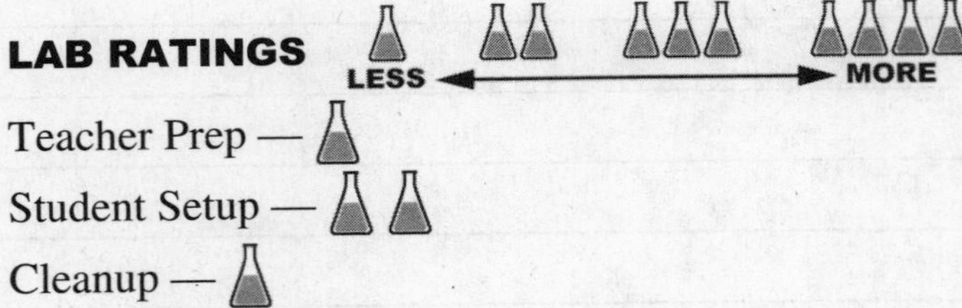

MATERIALS

For each group

- hair dryer
- plastic wrap, clear
- scissors
- shoe box
- tape
- thermometer, alcohol

For each student

- safety goggles

My Notes

SAFETY INFORMATION

Remind students to review all safety cautions and icons before beginning this lab. Instruct students to hold the hair dryer only by its handle, even when the switch is off. Have them unplug the hair dryer when it is not being used. Instruct students to hold the hair dryer at least 6 inches (in) from the shoe box and plastic wrap to prevent overheating. Tell students that they must immediately turn off their hair dryer if they observe any shrinking or melting of the plastic wrap.

TEACHER NOTES

In this activity, students will design a heating system that keeps the temperature of a shoe box, which represents the room of a home, between 24 degrees Celsius (°C) and 28 °C for 5 minutes (min). The hair dryer acts as the source of heat, and the thermometer gives the feedback necessary to determine when to switch the hair dryer on and off. Students will decide how to supply hot air to the shoe box (open the shoe box lid, cut a hole in the shoe box, and so forth). The thermometer inside the shoe box should remain visible at all times so that students can keep track of the temperature inside the box.

Tip This activity is designed to help students recognize the importance of control and feedback mechanisms in systems.

Student Tip Think of heating and air-conditioning systems in your family's home or car. Which systems work automatically? Which systems do you control manually?

Skills Focus Building Models, Drawing Conclusions, Identifying Constraints

MODIFICATION FOR DIRECTED *Inquiry*

Before beginning the activity, review the difference between manual and automatic controls. Tell students that they will construct a model of a heating system that uses manual controls. First, have students cut a hole in one end of a shoe box that allows air from the hair dryer to enter the box. Then have students remove the shoe box lid, place the thermometer in the box, and secure plastic wrap over the top of the box so that the thermometer is visible. Have students record their methods for maintaining the temperature of the shoe box.

Quick Lab continued

Answer Key

1. Accept all reasonable answers.
   Teacher Prompt How can you supply hot air to the shoe box without letting too much hot air leave the box? How can you keep the thermometer visible at all times?
2. Answers will vary.
3. Answers will vary.
4. The switch on the hair dryer acted as the control because it regulated when hot air was blown into the shoe box. Note: It is also correct to say that the human brain acted as the control because it decided when to flip the switch on the hair dryer.
   Teacher Prompt What regulated the amount of hot air added to the shoe box? What turned the heat source on and off?
5. The thermometer provided feedback.
   Teacher Prompt How did you know when to turn the hair dryer on and off?
6. Sample answer: The feedback influenced when the hair dryer was turned on and off. If the temperature was too low, the hair dryer was turned on. If the temperature was too high or within range, the hair dryer was turned off.
7. Sample answer: Automatic controls would allow the system to work when humans are not around. They would also make up for human error, such as loss of attention.

Name ______________________ Class ______________ Date ________________

QUICK LAB GUIDED Inquiry

Model a Home Heating System

Heating systems keep our homes, schools, and workplaces at a comfortable temperature. In this lab, you will design a heating system that keeps the temperature of a shoe box within a specified range. You will then describe the control and feedback mechanisms in your system. Remember that controls regulate systems and keep them efficient. Feedback mechanisms return information that may cause changes in the system.

OBJECTIVES

- Identify control and feedback mechanisms.
- Distinguish between manual and automatic controls.

MATERIALS

For each group:

- hair dryer
- plastic wrap, clear
- scissors
- shoe box
- tape
- thermometer, alcohol

For each student

- safety goggles

PROCEDURE

1. Look at the items your teacher has given you. With your group members, decide how to create a system that will keep the temperature of the shoe box between 24 degrees Celsius (°C) and 28 °C for 5 minutes (min). Record your procedure below.

____

____

____

____

____

____

2. Draw a sketch of what you think your system will look like.

____

____

____

____

____

____

3. After your teacher approves your procedure, carry it out. Record your observations.

____

____

____

____

Name ______________________ Class ______________ Date ______________

Quick Lab continued

4. What acted as the control in your system? Explain.

____

____

____

5. What provided the feedback in your system?

____

6. Did the feedback mechanism cause any changes in the system? If so, how?

____

____

____

7. Describe how automatic controls could improve your system.

____

____

____

____

QUICK LAB GUIDED *Inquiry*

Troubleshoot a Faulty System GENERAL

Small groups
15 minutes

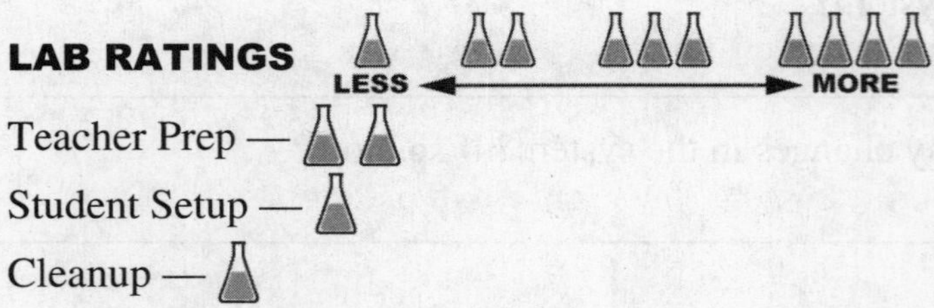

LAB RATINGS LESS ↔ MORE

Teacher Prep — 2
Student Setup — 1
Cleanup — 1

MATERIALS

For each group

- batteries, AA, AAA, C, or D, depending on the flashlight (4)
- flashlight
- flashlight bulb, replacement

For each student

- lab apron

SAFETY INFORMATION

Remind students to review all safety cautions and icons before beginning this lab. Note that batteries should be handled with care. Instruct students not to drop, cut, or try to open the batteries in any way.

My Notes

TEACHER NOTES

In this activity, students will identify problems with faulty flashlights and determine how to fix the flashlights as efficiently as possible. Before class begins, ensure that each flashlight has a problem that prevents it from working properly. For example, a flashlight may have a burned-out or missing light bulb, a dead battery, or batteries that are inserted incorrectly. Have students fix the flashlights using the spare batteries and light bulbs provided.

As a possible extension or replacement activity, have students troubleshoot a problem involving a series with a battery, electrical wire, and two light bulbs.

Tip This activity will help students understand how problems with subsystems can affect a larger system.

Student Tip Think about the parts of a flashlight. How can you test to see if these parts are working properly?

Skills Focus Identifying Problems, Drawing Conclusions

MODIFICATION FOR DIRECTED *Inquiry*

Review the parts of a flashlight with students. Help students brainstorm how some of these parts may cause problems with the flashlight. As a class, develop procedures for testing the flashlight for the problems discussed. Have student groups carry out these procedures and record their observations. After students have completed the activity, have them share with the class how they identified the problem with their flashlight and how they decided to fix it.

Quick Lab continued

Answer Key

1. Sample answer: The flashlight may have the wrong type of batteries in it. The flashlight may also have a burned-out light bulb.
   Teacher Prompt What are the parts of a flashlight? Which of these parts can you test or replace with the given materials?
2. Accept all reasonable answers.
3. Answers will vary.
4. Answers will vary.
5. Two subsystems within the flashlight are the batteries and the light bulb. If one of these subsystems fails, the flashlight will not work properly.
   Teacher Prompt How do flashlights produce light? How do flashlights get energy?
6. Sample answer: Systems analysis could be used to identify a problem with a car. For example, if a car won't start, a mechanic will need to determine which subsystem is failing: the engine, the battery, and so on.
   Teacher Prompt What are some machines that people need to have repaired?

Name ______________________ Class ______________ Date ________________

QUICK LAB GUIDED *Inquiry*

Troubleshoot a Faulty System

In this lab, you will use systems analysis to fix a broken flashlight. Systems analysis is the study of interacting systems. It allows analysts to see how a change to one part of a system affects one or multiple systems. A flashlight is considered a system because it has many components that work together to perform a function.

OBJECTIVES

- Use systems analysis to troubleshoot a system.
- Describe how systems interact.

MATERIALS

For each group

- batteries, AA, AAA, C, or D, depending on the flashlight (4)
- flashlight
- flashlight bulb, replacement

For each student

- lab apron

PROCEDURE

1. Describe some possible problems that may be causing your system to fail.

____

____

____

____

2. With your group members, develop procedures for testing your system for these problems.

____

____

____

____

____

____

3. After getting teacher approval, carry out your procedures. Record your observations below.

____

____

____

____

4. What was the problem with your system and how did you fix it?

____

____

____

Quick Lab continued

5. What are two subsystems within the flashlight? How can problems with these subsystems affect the flashlight as a whole?

____

____

____

6. Describe how systems analysis could be applied to another technological system.

____

____

____

S.T.E.M. LAB GUIDED *Inquiry* **AND** INDEPENDENT *Inquiry*

Design a Water Treatment System ADVANCED

Large Groups
45 minutes

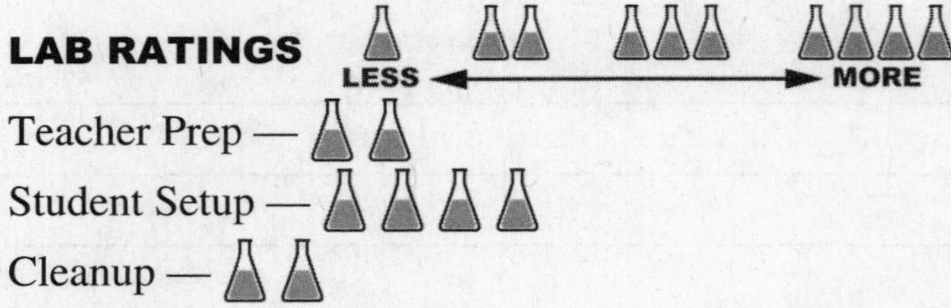

MATERIALS

For each group
- alum crystals, 20 g
- beaker (or jar)
- bottle, plastic 2 L with cap
- bottles, plastic 2 L, cut in half horizontally (2)
- containers, shallow (2)
- filter, coffee
- rock, small
- rubber band
- sand, coarse
- sand, fine
- spoon
- stopwatch (or clock with second hand)
- water, dirty, 1.5 L

For each student
- lab apron
- safety goggles

SAFETY INFORMATION

Remind students to review all safety cautions and icons before beginning this lab. Be sure that students wear safety goggles when working with their water purification apparatus. Instruct students to immediately clean up any water spills because slippery floors can be dangerous. Students must not taste any water treated by their purification systems because it is not safe to drink. Students should also not sniff the water directly. Demonstrate how students should detect odors by wafting them toward their nose. Have students wash and dry their hands at the completion of this activity.

TEACHER NOTES

In this activity, students will create a model water treatment system and test it on a sample of water. Student groups will devise procedures for the aeration, coagulation, sedimentation, and filtration processes typically found in water treatment plants. After you have approved students' procedures, allow them to carry out their plans. For the independent inquiry, allow students to select their own materials. Have several types and sizes of containers on hand from which students can choose. You should also provide alum crystals for the coagulation process.

Remember that 20 grams (g) of alum (potassium aluminum sulfate) is about 2 tablespoons (Tbls) and is an appropriate amount for 1.5 liters (L) of dirty water. Alum can be found in a pharmacy or in the spice section of the supermarket. It must be stirred into the water thoroughly to be most effective.

The volumes of sand and gravel given are approximate. You can use natural-color aquarium pebbles for the small rocks. To make dirty water, add 0.5 L dirt or mud to 5 L water.

Tip Use clear bottles and containers whenever possible so that students can observe the water from many angles.

My Notes

S.T.E.M. Lab continued

Skills Focus Devising Procedures, Constructing Models

MODIFICATION FOR DIRECTED Inquiry

Give students a procedure for developing a model water treatment system. For the aeration stage, have students pour the water from one container to another about a dozen times. For the coagulation stage, have students add alum to the water in an open container and stir thoroughly for about 5 minutes (min). For the sedimentation stage, have students allow the water to sit undisturbed, and then pour off the clearest water to a clean container. For the filtration stage, have students place a coffee filter inside the neck of a plastic bottle that has been cut in half. The bottle top should function like a funnel. Students should put pebbles and sand into the bottle neck and then slowly pour dirty water through the filter. Instruct students to record and share their observations at each stage.

Answer Key for GUIDED Inquiry

DEVELOP A PLAN

1. Accept all reasonable answers.
2. Sample answer: Inputs will be dirty water and alum crystals. Outputs will be cleaner water and separated impurities.
   Teacher Prompt What materials will you add to your system during the water treatment process? What materials will you end up with at the end of the process?
3. The goal of the water treatment system is to remove impurities from water.

BUILD A MODEL

4. Accept all reasonable answers.
5. Sample answer: The aerating removes some of the odor. The coagulation makes the solid material form into clumps so that it will settle out more easily, which happens during sedimentation. During filtering, the remaining solid material is removed.
   Teacher Prompt How has the water changed after being treated at each step?

ANALYZE RESULTS

6. Answers will vary.
7. Sample answer: There were no measurements that could be compared. Also, the sediment may need longer to settle.
   Teacher Prompt Did time constraints or the choice of materials affect your results? If so, how?

DRAW CONCLUSIONS

8. The system is open because it receives dirty water from the environment outside the system.
   Teacher Prompt Where do the inputs come from?

S.T.E.M. Lab continued

9. The subsystems interact through a common component: the dirty water. The output of one subsystem is the input of the next subsystem.
   Teacher Prompt What material or substance moves through all the subsystems in your system?
10. Sample answer: Each part of the system is important. Leaving out any one step will mean that the water will not be effectively cleaned. For example, if the sediment does not settle out, the material may clog the filter.

Connect TO THE ESSENTIAL QUESTION

11. Sample answer: Subsystems are organized in a way that allows the whole system to perform a function as efficiently as possible.

Answer Key for INDEPENDENT Inquiry

DEVELOP A PLAN

1. Accept all reasonable answers. Student answers should address each step.
2. Sample answer: Inputs will be dirty water and alum crystals. Outputs will be cleaner water and separated impurities.
   Teacher Prompt What materials will you add to your system during the water treatment process? What materials will you end up with at the end of the process?
3. The goal of the water treatment system is to remove impurities from water.
4. Sample answer: We will observe the appearance and odor of the water after each step has been completed.

BUILD A MODEL

5. Accept all reasonable answers.
6. Sample answer: The aerating removes some of the odor. The coagulation makes the solid material form into clumps so that it will settle out more easily, which happens during sedimentation. During filtering, the remaining solid material is removed.
   Teacher Prompt How has the water changed after being treated at each step?

ANALYZE RESULTS

7. Answers will vary.
8. Sample answer: There were no measurements that could be compared. Also, the sediment may need longer to settle.
   Teacher Prompt Did time constraints or the choice of materials affect your results? If so, how?

DRAW CONCLUSIONS

9. The system is open because it receives dirty water from the environment outside the system.
   Teacher Prompt Where do the inputs come from?

S.T.E.M. Lab continued

10. The subsystems interact through a common component: the dirty water. The output of one subsystem is the input of the next subsystem.
Teacher Prompt What material or substance moves through all the subsystems in your system?

11. Sample answer: Each part of the system is important. Leaving out any one step will mean that the water will not be effectively cleaned. For example, if the sediment does not settle out, the material may clog the filter.

Connect TO THE ESSENTIAL QUESTION

12. Sample answer: Subsystems are organized in a way that allows the whole system to perform a function as effectively as possible.

Name ______________________ Class ______________ Date ______________

S.T.E.M. LAB GUIDED Inquiry

Design a Water Treatment System

In this lab, you will design and build a model of a water treatment system. Most water treatment systems remove impurities from water through processes of aeration, coagulation, sedimentation, filtration, and disinfection. Aeration adds air to water and also allows gases trapped in the water to escape. Coagulation binds together solid particles that are suspended in the water so that they can be more easily removed. Alum is a chemical that can cause coagulation. Sedimentation occurs when solid particles, especially large particles or clumps, settle to the bottom of a liquid. Filtration removes small solid particles and can remove other impurities. Disinfectants kill organisms within the water.

OBJECTIVES

- Identify parts of a water treatment system.
- Describe how systems interact through common components.
- Distinguish between open systems and closed systems.

MATERIALS

For each group

- alum crystals, 20 g
- beaker (or jar)
- bottle, plastic 2 L with cap
- bottles, plastic 2 L, cut in half horizontally (2)
- containers, shallow (2)
- filter, coffee
- rock, small
- rubber band
- sand, coarse
- sand, fine
- spoon
- stopwatch (or clock with second hand)
- water, dirty, 1.5 L

For each student

- lab apron
- safety goggles

PROCEDURE

DEVELOP A PLAN

1 Determine how you can complete the aeration, coagulation, sedimentation, and filtration processes of a water treatment system using the materials provided. Consider using the following materials for each process:

aeration: bottom of plastic bottle (2)

coagulation: shallow plastic container, alum crystals, tablespoon

sedimentation: shallow plastic container

filtration: plastic bottle top, coffee filter, rubber band, fine sand, coarse sand,

Write a procedure for each step.

____

____

____

____

____

____

____

____

____

____

Name ______________________ Class ______________ Date ______________

S.T.E.M. Lab continued

2. What will be the inputs and outputs of your system?

___

3. What is the goal of your system?

___

BUILD A MODEL

4. With teacher approval, carry out your procedures. Observe the appearance and odor of the water after completing each step. Remember to waft the odor toward you with your hand. Do not sniff the water directly. Record your observations in the table below.

OBSERVATIONS OF WATER DURING TREATMENT

Treatment process	Observations
At start	
Aeration	
Coagulation	
Sedimentation	
Filtration	

5. How does each step help clean the water?

___

ANALYZE RESULTS

6. **Evaluating Results** Based on your results, what can you say about the effectiveness of your water treatment system?

___

Name ______________________ Class __________ Date ______________

S.T.E.M. Lab continued

7 **Identifying Constraints** What possible limits or sources of error might you expect in this investigation?

____

____

____

DRAW CONCLUSIONS

8 **Analyzing Models** Is your water treatment system an open system or a closed system? Explain.

____

____

____

____

9 **Describing Patterns** How do the steps, or subsystems, in your model interact?

____

____

____

____

10 **Making Predictions** Based on your data, what do you think would be the effect of leaving any one subsystem out of the water treatment system?

____

____

____

____

Connect TO THE ESSENTIAL QUESTION

11 **Explaining Concepts** Based on your experience with designing a water treatment system, describe how subsystems are organized within a larger system.

Name ______________________ Class ______________ Date ________________

S.T.E.M. LAB INDEPENDENT Inquiry

Design a Water Treatment System

In this lab, you will design and build a model of a water treatment system. Most water treatment systems remove impurities from water through processes of aeration, coagulation, sedimentation, filtration, and disinfection. Aeration adds air to water and also allows gases trapped in the water to escape. Coagulation binds together solid particles that are suspended in the water so that they can be more easily removed. Alum is a chemical that can cause coagulation. Sedimentation occurs when solid particles, especially large particles or clumps, settle to the bottom of a liquid. Filtration removes small solid particles and can remove other impurities. Disinfectants kill organisms within the water.

OBJECTIVES

- Identify parts of a water treatment system.
- Describe how systems interact through common components.
- Distinguish between open systems and closed systems.

MATERIALS

For each group

- alum crystals, 20 g
- beaker (or jar)
- bottle, plastic 2 L with cap
- bottles, plastic 2 L, cut in half horizontally (2)
- containers, shallow (2)
- filter, coffee
- rock, small
- rubber band
- sand, coarse
- sand, fine
- spoon
- stopwatch (or clock with second hand)
- water, dirty, 1.5 L

For each student

- lab apron
- safety goggles

PROCEDURE

DEVELOP A PLAN

1. Determine how you can complete the aeration, coagulation, sedimentation, and filtration processes of a water treatment system. Write a procedure for each step.

____

____

____

____

____

____

____

____

____

____

2. What will be the inputs and outputs of your system?

____

____

3. What is the goal of your system?

____

____

4. What data will you collect during your investigation?

BUILD A MODEL

5. With teacher approval, carry out your procedures. Make a table to show the data you collect during your investigation.

6. How does each step help clean the water?

ANALYZE RESULTS

7. **Evaluating Results** Based on your results, what can you say about the effectiveness of your water treatment system?

8. **Identifying Constraints** What possible limits or sources of error might you expect in this investigation?

S.T.E.M. Lab continued

DRAW CONCLUSIONS

9. **Analyzing Models** Is your water treatment system an open system or a closed system? Explain.

10. **Describing Patterns** How do the steps, or subsystems, in your model interact?

11. **Making Predictions** Based on your data, what do you think would be the effect of leaving any one subsystem out of the water treatment system?

Connect TO THE ESSENTIAL QUESTION

12. **Explaining Concepts** Based on your experience with designing a water treatment system, describe how subsystems are organized within a larger system.

QUICK LAB DIRECTED Inquiry

Tensile Strength Testing GENERAL

Small groups
30 minutes

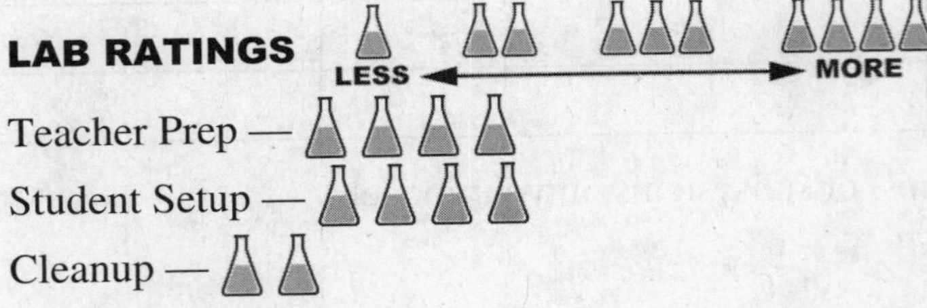

MATERIALS

For each group

- beaker, plastic 250 mL
- buckets, 5 gallon (2)
- clamps, small with greater than 1.5" jaw opening, "C" style or similar (2)
- material sample, plastic film "dogbone" shape, prepared
- rope (2 pieces)
- ruler, metric
- spring scale, including range 1000–2000 grams
- tub, large plastic
- water
- wood pieces with drilled holes, ¾" plywood, 10 cm × 10 cm (4)

For each student

- safety goggles

SAFETY INFORMATION

Remind students to review all safety cautions and icons before beginning this lab. Instruct students to suspend the upper clamp assembly above their face level so that if it moves during material failure it will not cause injury. Student should be very careful when hanging the apparatus from the support. Caution students to stand clear of the material as it falls, and to not place feet or other body parts under the falling bucket. Students should wear goggles to protect against unexpected material or setup failure.

TEACHER NOTES

In this activity, student will perform a material tensile strength test similar to those conducted in many industries, such as metal casting, textile, and plastics manufacturing.

To prepare for the lab, make a primary and a backup material sample for each group. For testing material, use four layers of flat plastic film, such as a newly unfolded garbage bag or trashcan liner, or plastic food wrap folded lengthwise. Trace "dogbone"-shaped testing samples on the material using a cardboard pattern made to the measurements shown in the diagram below, and cut out the four layers together. Note that plastics may be stronger in one direction than another, so samples cut from patterns oriented differently may have differing results. Mark each sample with two permanent marker dots 10 cm apart, centered on the narrow part of the sample.

My Notes

Quick Lab continued

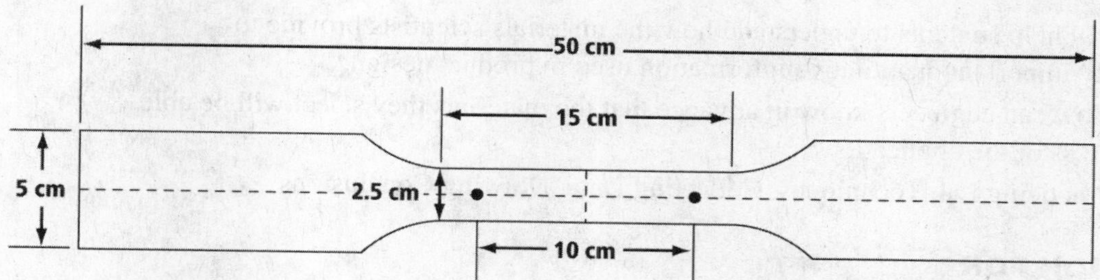

Also, prepare the wood pieces to be used for gripping the material ends by cutting them to size and drilling holes for the rope. The bowline is a good knot to use in the ropes.

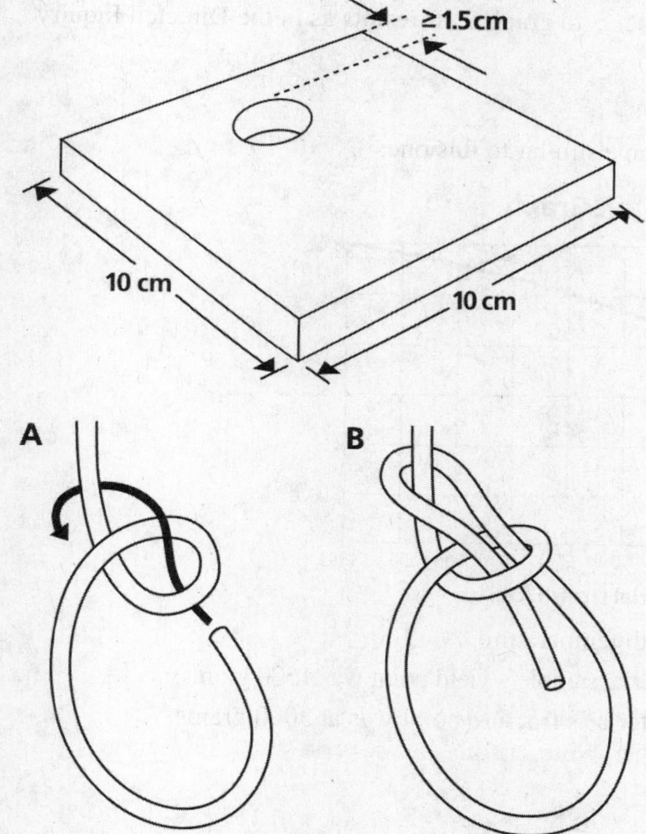

The lab may be conducted outside. Each group will require a sturdy support from which to hang the testing apparatus, such as a structural beam, a chin-up bar, or a tree limb. The support should be about 2 meters high to allow for material stretch. To save lab time, you can prepare the material samples in advance by clamping them between the upper wooden blocks and suspending them from the supports. The students can begin the lab by finding the mass of the lower blocks, clamp, and bucket before they are attached. You may wish to have students convert their mass data in grams to force in newtons before they construct their graphs.

Quick Lab continued

Tip This lab will help students to understand how the materials scientists provide to engineers supply important quantitative information used in product design.

Student Tip How can engineers know in advance that the materials they select will be able to handle the stress of the application?

Skills Focus Practicing Lab Techniques, Collecting Data, Drawing Conclusions

MODIFICATION FOR GUIDED Inquiry

For the Guided Inquiry option, provide the students with the same materials samples and equipment as in the Directed Inquiry, but instruct them to develop a plan to measure the elongation of the materials samples with increasing weight. Approve the plan for safety before they begin. Direct the students to graph their results as in the Directed Inquiry.

Answer Key

9. The graph should have a shape similar to this one:

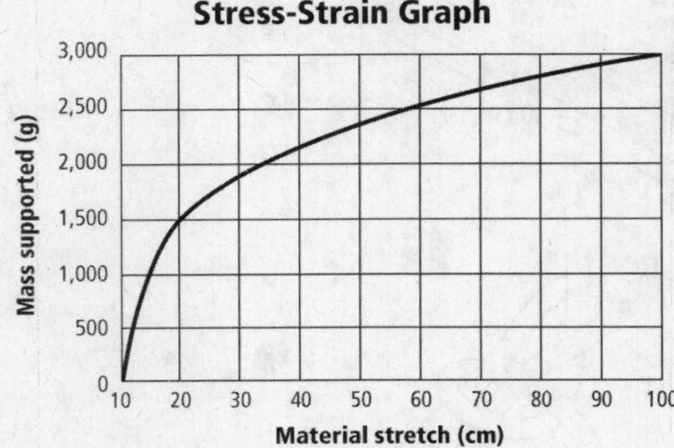

10. Note: Results may vary with temperature.

a. Sample answer: Our material sample's yield point was 1500 grams.

b. Sample answer: Our material's fracture point was at 3000 grams.

Name ______________________ Class ______________ Date ______________

QUICK LAB DIRECTED *Inquiry*

Tensile Strength Testing

In many industries, the strength of a material in tension is an important design consideration. In this lab, you will perform a tensile strength test similar to the ones materials engineers regularly conduct on the materials they develop. Unlike some other materials property tests, tensile testing is destructive to the sample.

OBJECTIVES

- Conduct a tensile strength test on plastic film material.

MATERIALS

For each group

- beaker, plastic 250 mL
- buckets, 5 gallon (2)
- clamps, small with greater than 1.5" jaw opening, "C" style or similar (2)
- material sample, plastic film "dogbone" shape, prepared
- rope (2 pieces)
- ruler, metric
- spring scale, including range 1000–2000 grams
- tub, large plastic
- water
- wood pieces with drilled holes, ¾" plywood, 10 cm × 10 cm (4)

For each student

- safety goggles

PROCEDURE

1. Use the spring scale to find the mass in grams (g) of one empty bucket, two wood pieces, one piece of rope, and one clamp. This will be the mass supported by the material sample at the start of the test. Write this value in the first cell of the table below.

Mass added to test system (g)	Distance between the dots on the sample (cm)	Total mass supported by the sample (g)
	10	0

Quick Lab continued

2 Prepare the sample for testing.

a. Position one end of the sample between two wood blocks, with the holes of the wood blocks aligned. Do not cover the holes with the sample. Position the clamp pads in the center of the wood blocks and the clamp body to the side of the sample. Tighten the C-clamp so that the end of the sample is firmly clamped between the two wood pieces. Make sure the sample will hang straight.

b. Pass one piece of rope through the holes in the wood block and hang the sample from the support as directed by your teacher.

c. Clamp the other end of the sample between the other two wood blocks, as above.

d. Pass the other rope through the lower wood block holes and hang one 5 gallon bucket from the rope.

3 Position the large plastic tub under the hanging bucket.

4 Measure the distance between the reference dots marked on the samples. They may have changed with the weight of the bucket. Record this measurement in the table.

Quick Lab continued

5. Use the beaker to add 250 milliliters (mL) of water to the hanging bucket. Pour the water in slowly and steadily. Record the mass added in the table. Remember that 250 mL of water is 250 grams (g) of mass.
6. Wait for a count of at least 10 to allow the material to stretch, and then use the ruler to measure the distance between the dots. If the distance is still changing, wait until it has stabilized to take the measurement. Record the value in the data table.
7. Repeat Steps 5 and 6 until the material fails.
8. In the data table, calculate the total mass supported by the material sample.
9. Graph your results on a separate sheet of paper.

   a. Use the middle column of the data table, the distance between the dots on the sample, for the *x*-axis values. The lowest value on the axis should be 10 centimeters (cm), the initial dot separation.

   b. Use the right column of the data table, the total mass supported by the sample, for the *y*-axis values. The lowest value on the *y*-axis should be 0.

   c. Your final graph should look like the sample graph shown below.

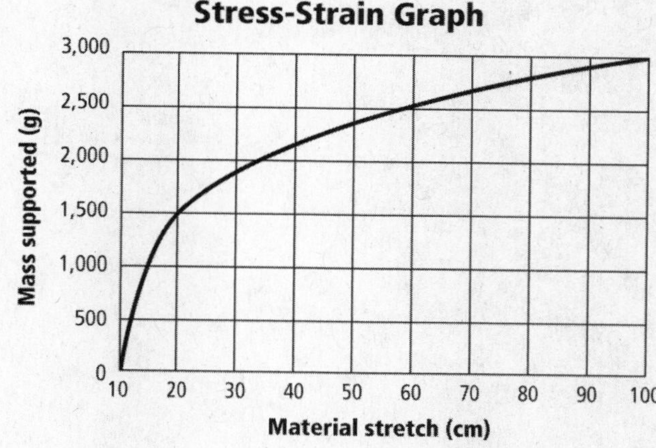

Quick Lab continued

10 The name for the type of plot that you made is a **stress-strain curve**. Its characteristic shape is similar for many kinds of materials such as metals and plastics.

a. The first part of the graph should be a straight line. During this part of the test, the material had **elastic deformation**. If you had taken the weight off of the sample during this phase, the material would have returned almost to its original shape. Write the maximum mass supported by your sample in the elastic deformation stage:

____

The point at which the graph begins to level out is called the **yield point.** Label the yield point on your graph.

b. The second part of your graph, where the curve levels out, is the **plastic deformation** stage. "Plastic" here does not mean the name of the material, but a nonreversible, permanent deformation (in this case, stretching). The plastic deformation stage ends when the material fails. Label the failure point on your graph. Write the maximum mass supported by your sample before it failed:

____

QUICK LAB DIRECTED *Inquiry*

Testing an Alloy GENERAL

Small groups
30 minutes

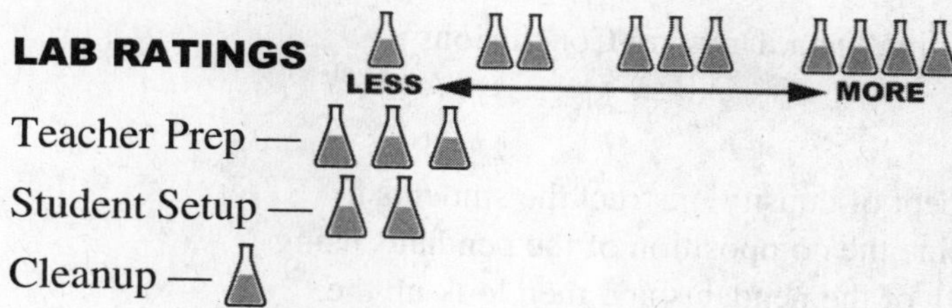

MATERIALS

For each group
- balance
- cylinder, graduated, 50 mL
- pennies (20)
- penny pendant, prepared
- sandpaper
- string (optional)
- twist tie (optional)
- water

For each student
- safety goggles

SAFETY INFORMATION

Remind students to review all safety cautions and icons before beginning this lab.

TEACHER NOTES

In this activity, students will explore nondestructive testing of materials. This lab takes advantage of the fact that pennies made from 1962 to 1981 are 95% copper and 5% zinc. A composition change was made during 1982. Pennies made in 1983 and later are 97.5% zinc and 2.5% copper. Because of their differences in composition, pennies from these two eras differ in density.

To prepare for the lab, construct a "pendant" for each group made from a stack of 15–20 post–1982 pennies glued together with a thin layer of strong waterproof glue, with the end pennies facing in to hide the year marks. Ask students to imagine that a customer ordered the pendant from a jeweler, and provided "ingots" of nearly pure copper to make them with. However, the customer suspects that the jeweler may have substituted a less valuable metal for the copper and merely plated the pendants on the outside with copper, keeping most of the copper for himself. The customer has asked the students to determine if this is the case, but without damaging the pendants in any way. Suggest to students that they use density as a means for testing.

Students will find that the density of the pendants is significantly less than that of the copper ingots, leading them to conclude that their pendant is indeed made mostly of another material.

When students have determined that the pendants are made of something other than copper, explain another nondestructive test for penny composition. A penny dropped onto a hard surface will make a dull "tuck" sound if it is mostly copper, but will make a metallic "tink" sound if it is mostly zinc. Allow students to conduct this test with sample pennies.

You can also provide students with sandpaper and allow them to scrape the edges of coins to see that there is a thin outer copper layer on the newer pennies. Point out that this would be considered "destructive testing." Do not allow them to scrape the pendants if you intend to re-use them.

My Notes

Quick Lab continued

Tip Zinc has a density that is about 80% of copper's. Provide larger pendants and more penny ingots to reduce the effects of measurement error.

Student Tip What if you wanted to know something about an object, but using the obvious way to find out would damage or destroy the object? You would look for another way to get the information. For example, you might want to find a way to test whether coins were inside a piggy bank without smashing it.

Skills Focus Practicing Lab Techniques, Collecting Data, Drawing Conclusions

MODIFICATION FOR GUIDED Inquiry

After ensuring that students understand the concept of density, instruct the students to develop a plan for using the materials to determine the composition of the pendants using density. For example, they might find the density of the pendants and then look up the expected value for copper. Approve plans before students begin.

Answer Key

1. Measurements will vary. Sample data:

DENSITY OF PENNIES

Mass of pendant (g)	Volume of water (mL)	Volume of water plus pendant (mL)	Volume of pendant (cm^3)	Density of pendant (g/cm^3)
46.2	24.0	29.5	5.5	8.4

2. Measurements will vary. Sample data:

DENSITY OF THE PENDANT

Mass of pendant (g)	Volume of water (mL)	Volume of water plus pendant (mL)	Volume of pendant (cm^3)	Density of pendant (g/cm^3)
32.8	26.0	30.5	4.5	7.3

3. Calculations will vary. Sample answer: The percent difference = 100 × (8.4 – 7.3)/ 8.4 = 13%. This is a large difference.
4. Sample answer: The pendant must be made of a different material from the copper pennies because it has a lower density.
5. Sample answers: The new pennies made a different sound, more like a high-pitched "ting" than a "tuck" sound. When I scraped the edge of the new penny across the sandpaper, there was a silvery metal under the copper layer. For the old penny, there was just shinier copper.

Name ______________________ Class ______________ Date ______________

QUICK LAB DIRECTED *Inquiry*

Testing an Alloy

Manufacturers generally want to test the properties of their finished products to make sure the products meet specifications. However, manufacturers often do not want to damage the product during the testing. In this activity, you will use a nondestructive testing technique to analyze the composition of a product and use the information to draw conclusions about whether the product meets specifications.

OBJECTIVE

- Determine the composition of an object by measuring its density.

MATERIALS

For each group

- balance
- cylinder, graduated, 50 mL
- pennies (20)
- penny pendant, prepared
- sandpaper
- string (optional)
- twist tie (optional)
- water

For each student

- safety goggles

PROCEDURE

1. Assume that pennies are made of copper. Find the density of copper using the pennies provided.
   a. Measure the mass of the pennies as a group and record the data in the table on the next page.
   b. Place enough water in the graduated cylinder to fill it about halfway. Measure the volume of the water to the nearest 0.5 milliliter (mL). Be sure to place the graduated cylinder on a flat surface and read the bottom of the liquid meniscus in the cylinder. Look straight across the meniscus as shown in the diagram.

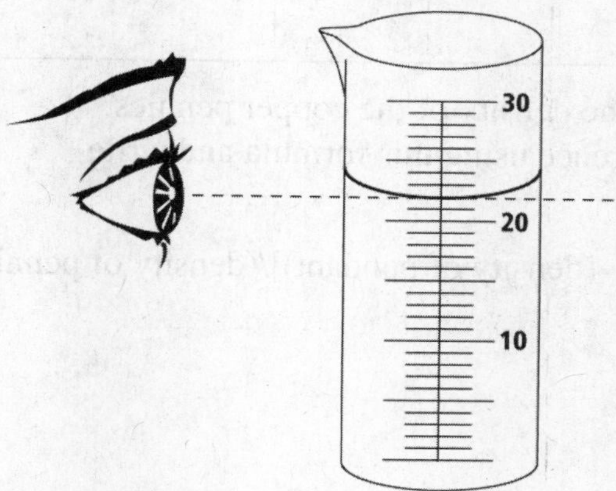

   c. Carefully add the pennies to the water in the graduated cylinder, making sure not to allow any water to splash out while you make your additions. For easier retrieval, you may attach a string or twist tie to the pennies and then lower the pennies into the water.Measure the volume of the water plus the pennies to the nearest 0.5 mL.
   d. Calculate the volume of the pennies by taking the difference between the volume without pennies and the volume with pennies. Remember that 1 mL is equal to 1 cm^3.

Name ____________________ Class ____________ Date ____________

Quick Lab continued

e. Calculate the density of the copper pennies by dividing the mass in grams by the volume in cubic centimeters. Record your calculated density for copper in the table below.

DENSITY OF PENNIES

Mass of pennies (g)	Volume of water (mL)	Volume of water plus pennies (mL)	Volume of pennies (cm^3)	Density of pennies (g/cm^3)

2. Next, find the density of the pendant. Remove the twist tie and the string, if used.
   a. Measure the mass of the pendant and record it in the table below.
   b. Measure the volume of the pendant using the same water displacement method you used for the pennies. Record your results in the table.
   c. Calculate the density of the pendant. Record your result in the table.

DENSITY OF THE PENDANT

Mass of pendant (g)	Volume of water (mL)	Volume of water plus pendant (mL)	Volume of pendant (cm^3)	Density of pendant (g/cm^3)

3. Compare the density of the pendant with the density of the copper pennies. Express the comparison as a percent difference using this formula and write your result below.

   % difference = 100 ×[(density of pennies)–(density of pendant)]/(density of pennies)

Name ______________________ Class ____________ Date ______________

Quick Lab continued

4. Do you think that the pendant is made from the same material as the copper pennies? Explain why or why not.

____

____

5. Your teacher will now give you some additional information and materials for further testing. Record your observations and comments below.

____

____

____

____

____

QUICK LAB DIRECTED *Inquiry*

Natural and Artificial Insulation GENERAL

Small groups
30 minutes

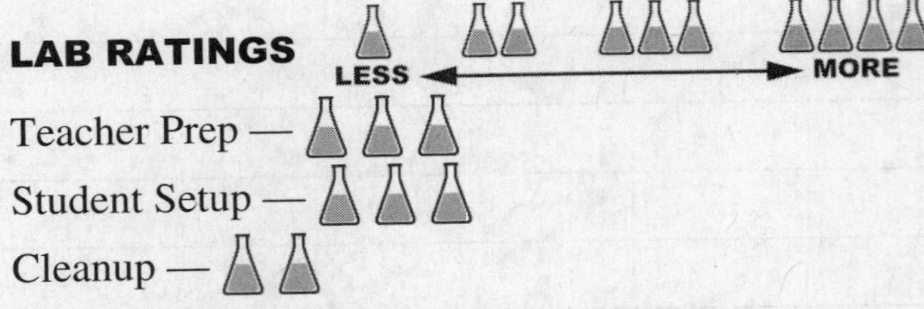

SAFETY INFORMATION

Remind students to review all safety cautions and icons before beginning this lab. If fiberglass insulation is used as one of the insulating materials, the teacher should prepare that sample in advance while wearing goggles and protective gloves and seal it between the bag layers. Students should not handle the fiberglass insulation directly. Have paper towels available to clean up spilled water.

TEACHER NOTES

In this activity, students will compare the thermal conductivity of biological insulating materials with that of human-made insulating materials, noting their common characteristics. Although manufactured insulation is often made from raw natural materials, for the purposes of the lab, "human-made" indicates a material that is highly processed as compared to its natural state.

To prepare for the lab, use the list of suggested materials below to provide a sample of insulating material for each group. Be sure to include both natural and human-made samples from across the range of thermal conductivity from air to water. Sheet materials should be cut to size. For other types of insulating samples, collect about 500 mL of material. Prepare enough water at 37 °C for all groups using insulating material.

Students will work in small groups. One group will be the control, testing with no insulating material; the other groups will each work with a different insulating material. Each group will fill the space between the layers of the two nested plastic bags with insulating material. Students will add the 37 °C water and a thermometer to the inner bag. They will then place the bag system in a pan of ice water and measure the temperature drop over 10 minutes. They will add ice to the pan as necessary to keep its temperature, measured by the second thermometer, constant at approximately 5–7 °C.

MATERIALS

For each group
- bags, plastic zip-top (2)
- beakers, 250 mL (3)
- dishpan, plastic
- ice
- insulating material sample (15 cm x 25 cm sheet or approx. 500 mL volume)
- stapler or strong tape (for use with sheet material only)
- thermometers, alcohol (2)
- watch or clock
- water, 37 °C

For each student
- lab apron
- safety goggles

My Notes

Quick Lab continued

The groups will then pool their data for analysis. Students will order the materials by performance and make a column graph of the results. Students will examine the materials and report on their common physical properties.

Tip This activity may help students understand how the characteristics of natural materials can inform the design of human-made materials manufactured for a similar purpose.

Student Tip How are materials manufactured for insulation similar to materials that provide natural insulation for organisms?

Skills Focus Making Observations, Analyzing Data, Making Graphs

MODIFICATION FOR GUIDED *Inquiry*

- Prior to the day of the lab, introduce the students to the general lab plan and invite them to bring in samples of insulating materials for testing. Provide or have them research the published values for thermal conductivity for each material. During the activity, encourage students to make predictions and then compare their test results with what might be expected (lower thermal conductivity should result in a slower temperature drop).
- Offer the students the use of a microscope for a closer look at the physical properties of the materials.
- For a qualitative activity, instead of measuring the temperature of water in the inner bag, students may also place their hands inside the inner bag to feel the protective effect of the insulation.

The table below lists suggested insulating materials and their approximate thermal conductivities when dry, if applicable. The values for air and water are included for reference. Included also are values for dolphin and whale blubber; these may be compared with wetsuit material and vegetable shortening, respectively. Note: students tend to be particularly intrigued with the performance of vegetable shortening.

THERMAL CONDUCTIVITY ($WM^{-1}K^{-1}$)

Natural materials	Human-made or highly processed material
Air 0.03	Reflective bubble wrap insulation 0.03
Down 0.03	Styrofoam 0.03
Rabbit fur 0.03	Fiberglass or rockwool insulation 0.04 (handled by teacher only)
Wool 0.04	
Balsa 0.05	
Corkboard 0.04	
Wool felt 0.07	
Sawdust 0.08	
Cotton 0.09	Synthetic fleece 0.08
Straw 0.09	
Dolphin blubber 0.15	Neoprene wetsuit material 0.15 (0.45 when compressed at depth)
Soil with organic material 0.15	
Rubber 0.16	
Oil, olive 0.17	Mineral oil 0.14
Minke whale blubber 0.25	Vegetable shortening 0.22
Water 0.60	

Quick Lab continued

Answer Key

7. Accept all reasonable answers.

8. Accept all reasonable answers.

9. Graphs should match the class data.

10. Answers will vary but should match the class data.

11. Answers will vary but should match the class data.

12. Accept all reasonable answers. Sample answer: The wool felt and the synthetic fleece look and feel similar. They are both made of curly tangled fibers and have a similar texture.

13. Sample answer: The natural and the human-made insulation material have the same purpose. They do the same job in the same way. The idea for the human-made insulation may have come from the natural insulation.

14. Sample answer: The structure of both the natural and the human-made materials traps air and keeps it from moving around.
Teacher Prompt Still air is an excellent thermal insulator.

Name ______________________ Class ______________ Date ______________

QUICK LAB DIRECTED *Inquiry*

Natural and Artificial Insulation

Humans and many animals need to keep their internal body temperature within a certain range to survive. However, often the temperature of the surrounding environment is outside this range. To provide protection from hot or cold temperatures, organisms have physical adaptations that keep them insulated. People have developed many types of insulation products based on these natural adaptations. In this activity, you will examine and test natural and artificial insulating materials.

OBJECTIVE

- Compare the characteristics and performance of different insulating materials, natural and human-made.

MATERIALS

For each group

- bags, plastic zip-top (2)
- beakers, 250 mL (3)
- dishpan, plastic
- ice
- insulating material sample (15 cm x 25 cm sheet or approx. 500 mL volume)
- stapler or strong tape (for use with sheet material only)
- thermometers, alcohol (2)
- watch or clock
- water, 37 °C

For each student

- lab apron
- safety goggles

PROCEDURE

1. Fill the dishpan or similar container with at least 1.5 L of cold tap water. Place about a dozen ice cubes and one of the thermometers in the water. Throughout the activity, add ice as necessary to keep the water at 0°–10° C.

2. If your group is the "control" group, you will be testing without insulation. It will be assumed that the thin single plastic bag you will use has no insulating properties. Your group will not use a second bag.

Name ______________________ Class ______________ Date ______________

Quick Lab continued

3 If your teacher has given you a sample of insulation, prepare it for testing:

a. If your sample is a sheet of insulating material, fold it in half and staple or tape the sides together, as shown. Do not fasten across the top.

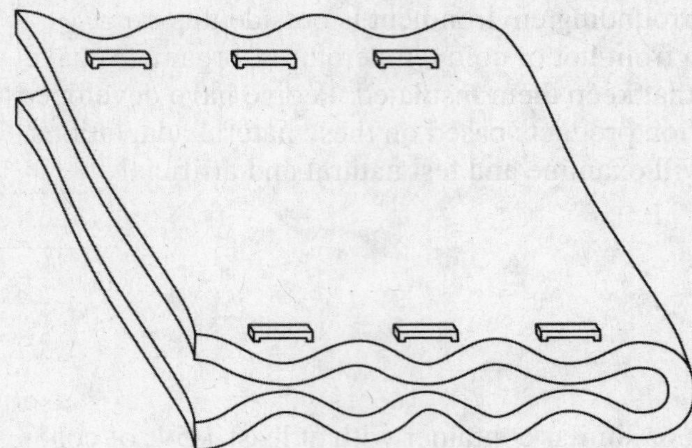

b. If your sample is a liquid or another material that is not in a sheet, measure out approximately 500 mL of the sample and place the sample inside one of the clear plastic sandwich bags.

4 If you are using an insulating material, turn a second plastic bag inside out and slip it inside the first bag. Seal the inner bag to the outer bag. (The bags will not seal completely at the corners.) The insulating material should now be held between the layers of the two bags. If necessary, distribute the insulating material so that its thickness is about the same on the sides and bottom. The two bags should form a "pocket" with an opening in the top.

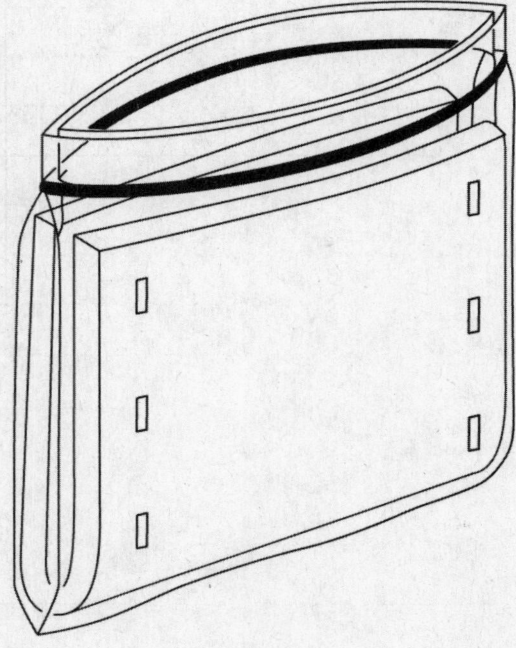

Quick Lab continued

5. Add 250 mL of water at 37 °C to the inner bag. Place the second thermometer in the inner bag also.

6. Place the bag system in the ice water and hold it vertically so that the water levels inside the inner bag and in the ice water are the same. Do not allow ice water to flow into the inner bag or the space between bags.

7. Start the stopwatch. After 10 minutes, note the temperature of the water inside the bag. Record your results below:

   Material: ______________________

   Initial temperature of water, °C: ______________________

   Final temperature of water, °C: ______________________

   Calculate: Temperature drop, °C: ______________________

8. Report your value for the temperature drop to the class. When all groups have reported their temperature drops, copy the information here, including the temperature drop found by your group:

Material										
Temperature Change, °C										

9. Order the data from largest to smallest and make a column graph on the grid provided below. Be sure to label each column with the name of the material.

Insulation Performance

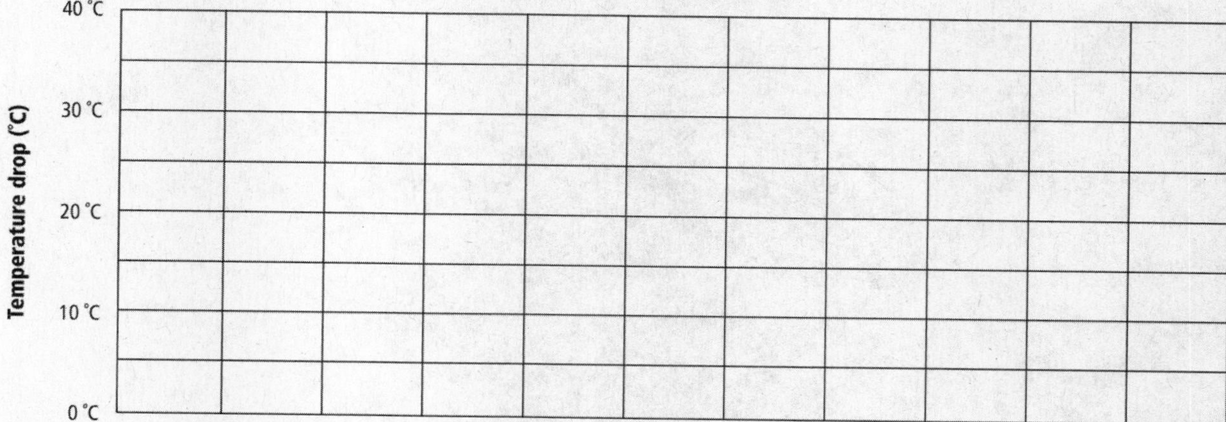

Material name

10. Which material allowed the smallest drop in temperature?

____

Quick Lab continued

11 Which material allowed the largest drop in temperature?

____

12 Examine the materials used by all of the groups. Select a pair of similar materials, one natural and one human-made. Describe the physical features that are common to both:

____

____

____

____

13 Why do you think the processed material is similar to the natural material?

____

____

14 How do the best-performing natural and human-made materials tested accomplish their purpose?

____

____

QUICK LAB GUIDED *Inquiry*

Yeast Gas Production GENERAL

Pairs or small groups
45 minutes

LAB RATINGS LESS ⟷ MORE

Teacher Prep — 4
Student Setup — 4
Cleanup — 3

SAFETY INFORMATION

Remind students to review all safety cautions and icons before beginning this lab. Do not allow students to insert the glass tubing into the rubber stoppers; instead, prepare the stoppers in advance using instructions below. Paper towels should be available to clean up spilled water.

TEACHER NOTES

In this lab, students will work in pairs or small groups to investigate the conditions required by yeast for gas production.

As part of the lab preparation, prepare the rubber stoppers with the glass tubing. To insert glass tubing into a rubber stopper, protect your hands with leather gloves. Check that the hole is the correct size and lubricate it with glycerin or soapy water. Hold the glass close to the stopper. Twist gently to guide the glass through the stopper as you push.

Also, before the lab, you will need to "proof" the yeast according to the package directions to be sure that it is alive and fresh. Run a test of the lab setup to check that the proportions of yeast and sugar and the water temperature used in the standard experiment work well with your brand of yeast; adjust as necessary.

For ease in sharing results, post large versions of Table 1 and Table 2 in the classroom for a student from each group to fill in as experiments are completed.

Introduce the lab with a description of yeast as an organism and in its applications for human purposes. Points to include:

- Yeast is a member of the Fungi kingdom.
- Humans use some species of yeast in consumable products, such as for leavening bread and fermenting beer and wine. Also, naturally present and usually harmless yeast can sometimes cause disease if it gets out of control.
- Basic bread dough consists of flour, water, salt, and yeast. Yeast converts sugar in dough to carbon dioxide, which causes small pockets of gas in the dough and expands it. The yeast die when the dough is baked, and the small pockets become baked in place.

MATERIALS

For the class
- thermometer, alcohol

For each group
- beaker, 250 mL
- dishpan, 2 L
- flasks, Erlenmeyer, 250 mL (2)
- funnel, small plastic
- graduated cylinders, 100 mL or larger (2)
- plastic wrap
- rubber band
- salt
- spoons, metric measuring
- stirring sticks, wooden (2)
- stoppers, rubber, one hole opening with rigid tube connector (2)
- stopwatch
- sugar
- tape
- tubing, rubber or plastic, 1 m (2 pieces)
- water, 37–43 °C
- yeast, active dry

For each student
- lab apron
- safety goggles

Quick Lab continued

- The baking term "to leaven" refers to using an agent, such as baking powder, baking soda, or yeast, to produce small gas bubbles throughout bread dough to make it rise.

Each group will simultaneously do one directed standard experiment and one of their own design. For the standard experiments, each group will use 5 mL dry yeast and 15 mL sugar in the first flask; assign half the groups to also add 5 mL of salt to their first flask. For the student-designed group experiments, students decide what proportion of warm water, sugar, yeast, and/or salt to put in the second flasks.

Prepare a pitcher of warm water at about 37 °C –43 °C. When each group is ready, pour 250 mL into each group's beakers. This ensures that all experiments use approximately the same temperature water. Each group will add 100 mL of water to the first flask and the predetermined amount of water to the second flask, stir, and put in the rubber stoppers. Students will record the time required for the yeast to produce 100 mL of carbon dioxide in each inverted graduated cylinder. The groups will pool their results at the end for analysis.

Tip Ensure students understand that the gas produced from yeast is the result of a living organism's process, unlike gas produced from chemical leavening agents such as baking powder.

Skills Focus Practicing Lab Techniques, Devising Procedures, Collecting Data

MODIFICATION FOR INDEPENDENT *Inquiry*

As a modification for independent inquiry, instruct the students in how to use the gas collection apparatus and provide them with the basic dry ingredients and equipment. Students will design and carry out a series of experiments to determine the optimum proportions and water temperature for carbon dioxide gas production. In an expanded activity, additional materials such as flour, vinegar, potato water, apple juice, or milk could also be made available.

Answer Key

12. Sample answer: The experiments that included salt took longer to fill the cylinders to 100 mL. The salt seemed to have a slowing-down effect on the production of gas.

13. Answers will vary. Sample answer: Some combinations didn't seem to work at all. One combination, with twice as much yeast as the standard recipe, seemed to work better than the standard recipe. Any recipe with salt in it seemed to have much less gas production.

Name ______________________ Class ______________ Date ______________

QUICK LAB GUIDED *Inquiry*

Yeast Gas Production

Humans make use of other organisms for many purposes. For thousands of years, people have leavened bread using the fact that when yeast consumes sugars, it produces carbon dioxide gas. In this activity, you will investigate the conditions yeast needs to produce this gas.

OBJECTIVE

- Observe the gas produced from two different proportions of ingredients mixed with yeast.

MATERIALS

For the class
- thermometer

For each group
- beaker, 250 mL
- dishpan, 2 L capacity or similar
- flasks, Erlenmeyer, 250 mL (2)
- funnel, small plastic
- graduated cylinders, 100 mL or larger (2)
- plastic wrap
- rubber band
- salt
- stirring sticks, wooden (2)
- spoons, metric measuring
- stoppers, rubber, one hole opening with rigid tube connector (2)
- stopwatch
- sugar
- tape
- tubing, rubber or plastic, 1 m (2 pieces)
- water, warm
- yeast, active dry

For each student
- lab apron
- safety goggles

PROCEDURE

You will be conducting two experiments simultaneously. In one experiment, you will mix yeast with a standard "recipe" of ingredients. In the other, you will work with your group to decide which, and how much, of the ingredients to use.

1. Build the gas collection setup. Fill the dishpan with at least 1.5 L of water. Completely submerge a graduated cylinder. Then gently turn the cylinder so that the cylinder is upside down in the pan and the cylinder remains full of water. There should be little or no air in the cylinder (<1 mL). Carefully place the cylinders along one side of the water pan. Use a clip and a rubber band to hold the cylinder against the side of the pan. Repeat this process for a second graduated cylinder.

2. Working underwater, place one end of a tubing piece in each graduated cylinder, pushing it at least halfway up into the cylinder. Carefully connect the free ends of the tubing to the glass tubes in the rubber stoppers.

3. Prepare the "standard" flask with the dry ingredients. Using the funnel and the measuring spoons, add 5 mL dry yeast and 15 mL sugar. Additionally, some groups will add 5 mL of salt as directed by your teacher. Write the ingredients and their amounts on a small piece of paper, and attach it to the flask with tape.

Quick Lab continued

4. Prepare your group's experimental flask with the dry ingredients. Work with your group to decide how much yeast, sugar, salt, and water to use. You do not have to use all of the available ingredients. Write all ingredients and their amounts on a small piece of paper. Have your teacher approve your plan and initial your paper, and then add your measured dry ingredients to the second flask. Attach the paper to the flask to label it.

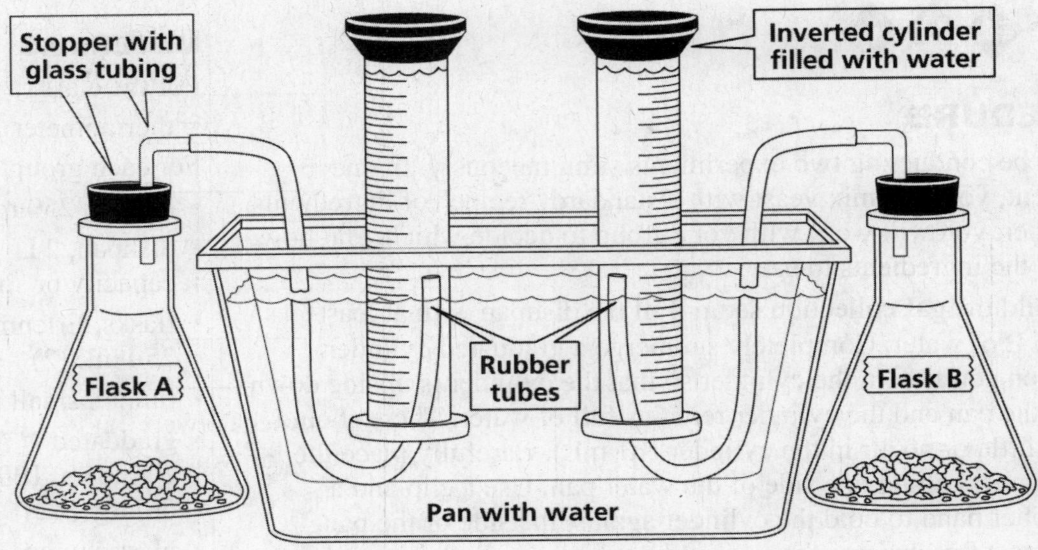

5. When all groups are ready, your teacher will pour water at approx. 37 °C – 43 °C into each group's 250 mL beakers. Read Steps 6–8 before using the water.

6. Add 100 mL of the water to the standard flask and your predetermined amount to the experimental flask. Using the wooden stirring stick, briskly stir the ingredients for 30 seconds to dissolve the yeast and sugar.

7. Place the rubber stoppers connected to the tubing in the flasks, making sure to not disturb the tubing in the cylinders.

8. Start the stopwatch.

9. Observe the gas bubbling up into the cylinders. As the cylinders fill, hold them vertically in the water so they do not float up, and so that you can measure the volume of the gas produced.

10. As each cylinder fills to 100 mL with carbon dioxide, note the time on the stopwatch. Record your results in Table 1 and Table 2 in Step 11.

11. Share your results with the other groups. Record the results for the standard experiment in Table 1 and the results for each group's experiments in Table 2.

Quick Lab continued

TABLE 1: STANDARD EXPERIMENTS (5 ML YEAST, 15 ML SUGAR, 100 ML WATER)

Group	1	2	3	4	5	6
Included 5 mL salt?						
Time to 100 mL CO_2, min:sec						

TABLE 2: GROUP EXPERIMENTS

Group	1	2	3	4	5	6
Yeast, mL						
Sugar, mL						
Salt, mL						
Water, mL						
Time to 100 mL CO_2, min:sec						

12 For the standard experiments, compare the gas production times between the experiments with and without added salt. What effect, if any, do you think the salt had on the gas production?

____

____

____

____

____

____

13 For the group experiments, comment on any patterns you see among the results from the various combinations of ingredients.

____

____

____

____

____

____

QUICK LAB GUIDED *Inquiry*

Inventor Trading Cards BASIC

Small groups
20 minutes/day for 2 days

LAB RATINGS LESS ← → MORE

Teacher Prep — 2
Student Setup — 1
Cleanup — 1

MATERIALS

For each group
- glue
- Internet or library resources
- paper, card stock (or poster board)
- pens, black ink
- sample trading card

My Notes

TEACHER NOTES

In this activity, students will work in small groups to design trading cards for inventors that have advanced science or contributed to society. On Day 1, have students choose an inventor (or team of inventors). Examples of inventors include, but are not limited to, Katherine Blodgett, George Washington Carver, Stephanie Kwolek, Ellen Ochoa, Arthur L. Schawlow and Charles H. Townes, Grace Hopper, Kenneth Matsumura, Aron Losonczi, Valeria Thomas, and Tim Berners-Lee. Students should use the Internet or library resources to gather information and create their cards. When students have finished, collect their cards and make photocopies for the other students in the class. On Day 2, have students present their cards. Distribute the photocopied cards to the class.

To prepare for the activity, create or obtain a model trading card that students can use to help them determine what information to include on their own cards.

Tip If students need more time, you may allow them to complete their cards and plan their presentations for homework.

Student Tip Choose reliable Internet sites for your research. Sites should list an author and references.

Skills Focus Conducting Research, Organizing Information

MODIFICATION FOR INDEPENDENT *Inquiry*

Have students plan an investigation inspired by the work of their inventor. Students should identify materials and devise procedures for their investigations, considering the materials and space available in the classroom. Have students explain how their investigation would advance scientific knowledge. As an extension activity, allow students to proceed with all reasonable investigations. Invite students to share their findings with the class with a poster or presentation.

Quick Lab continued

Answer Key

2. Accept all reasonable answers.
3. Accept all reasonable answers. Students should explain that technological systems are part of the designed world. These technologies advance science and improve people's quality of life.
   Teacher prompt Have these inventions improved people's quality of life? Are they the products of engineers and scientists?
4. Accept all reasonable answers. Students should cite reasons such as meeting people's needs, solving problems, or improving upon existing technology.

Name ______________________ Class ______________ Date ________________

QUICK LAB GUIDED *Inquiry*

Inventor Trading Cards

In this lab, you will research an inventor or team of inventors that has advanced science or contributed to society. You will use the information you gather to create a trading card for your inventor.

OBJECTIVES

- Explain how engineers and scientists have contributed to the designed world.
- Identify reasons why technology is developed.

MATERIALS

For each group

- glue
- Internet or library resources
- paper, card stock (or poster board)
- pens, black ink
- sample trading card

PROCEDURE

1. Choose an inventor from the list provided by your teacher, or ask your teacher to approve a different inventor of your choosing.
2. Decide what information you need to include on your inventor trading card. Write the information you plan to include in the space below.

   ____
   ____
   ____
   ____
   ____
   ____

3. Use the Internet or library resources to find information about your inventor and his or her inventions. Are these inventions part of the designed world? Explain.

   ____
   ____
   ____
   ____
   ____
   ____

Quick Lab continued

4. Why did your inventor develop the technology he or she did?

____

____

____

____

____

____

5. Create the trading card. Include the information you identified in Step 2. If possible, include a picture of your inventor or one of his or her inventions on the front of the card. Give your completed card to your teacher.

6. Present your card to the class. Explain the most important facts about your inventor and his or her inventions. Make sure to discuss how your inventor contributed to the designed world.

QUICK LAB INDEPENDENT *Inquiry*

Investigate Energy Efficiency GENERAL

Small groups
20 minutes

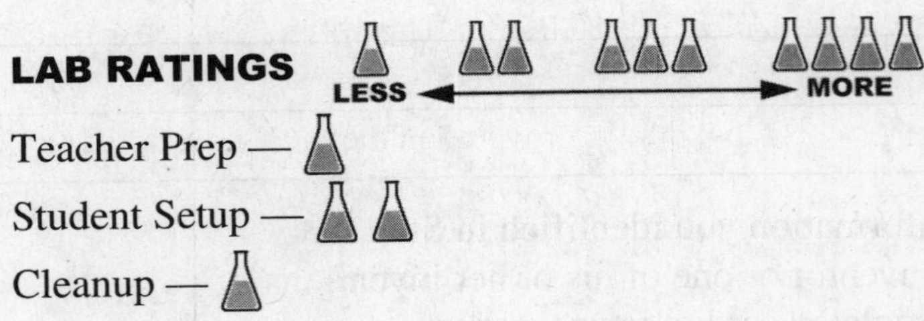

LAB RATINGS

Teacher Prep —
Student Setup —
Cleanup —

MATERIALS

For each group

- lamps, goose-neck (2) (or table lamps)
- light bulb, compact fluorescent
- light bulb, incandescent
- ruler, metric
- thermometers (2)

For each student

- safety goggles

SAFETY INFORMATION

Remind students to review all safety cautions and icons before beginning this lab. Instruct students not to touch light bulbs while they are on. Students should not unscrew the lightbulbs unless they have completely cooled.

TEACHER NOTES

In this lab, students will investigate whether an incandescent or a compact fluorescent light bulb is more energy efficient. Provide materials for students to use in their investigations, but allow them to devise their own procedures.

Tip Encourage students to use what they learn from this lab to discuss energy efficiency in their homes with a parent or guardian.

Skills Focus Devising Procedures, Practicing Lab Techniques

My Notes

MODIFICATION FOR GUIDED *Inquiry*

Using input from students, develop a procedure for the investigation as a class. For example, students may place the incandescent light bulb in one lamp and the compact fluorescent light bulb in the other. Students may then place one thermometer under each lamp so that both thermometers are the same distance from the light bulb. Then, students may record the temperature of the thermometers after five minutes to determine which light bulb gives off less heat. Have student groups carry out the procedure. Students should identify the variables in the experiment and design a table in which to record their data.

Quick Lab continued

Answer Key

2. Accept all reasonable answers.
3. Sample answer: Observations should show that the incandescent light bulb emits more heat.
   Teacher Prompt What is one variable that can indicate a light bulb is wasting energy? How can you measure this variable?
4. Sample answer: The fluorescent light bulb is more efficient because it gives off less heat. Therefore, it uses less energy to produce the same amount of light.
5. Sample answer: The fluorescent light bulb was developed to improve upon the incandescent light bulb, which is not very efficient. Fluorescent light bulbs can help the environment because they use less energy. As a result, limited energy resources, such as fossil fuels, are conserved.
   Teacher Prompt Why are new technologies developed? Which of these reasons explains why the compact fluorescent light bulb was developed?
6. Sample answer: This information may lead individuals to choose more efficient light bulbs for their homes. It could also cause political leaders to make laws about using more efficient light bulbs.
7. Sample answer: A light bulb is an example of technology because it is a designed product that serves a purpose in our society.
   Teacher Prompt What is technology? Is technology natural or designed?

Name ______________________ Class ______________ Date ________________

QUICK LAB INDEPENDENT *Inquiry*

Investigate Energy Efficiency

Some light bulbs have very low energy efficiency. Most of the energy they use is emitted as heat instead of light. In this lab, you will investigate whether an incandescent or a compact fluorescent light bulb is more energy efficient. As you plan your investigation, consider how to measure which type of light bulb emits more heat.

OBJECTIVES

- Identify reasons why technology is developed.
- Describe how technology can affect the environment.
- Describe how environmental concerns can influence decisions about technology.

MATERIALS

For each group

- lamps, goose-neck (2) (or table lamps)
- light bulb, compact fluorescent
- light bulb, incandescent
- ruler, metric
- thermometers (2)

For each student

- safety goggles

PROCEDURE

1. You will investigate the following question: Which type of light bulb, incandescent or compact fluorescent, is more energy efficient? Discuss your ideas in your group.

2. Devise a procedure to investigate the question from Step 1. Consider the materials you have available.

____

____

____

____

____

____

____

____

3. With your teacher's approval, carry out your procedure. Record your observations in the space below.

Quick Lab continued

4 Which light bulb is more energy efficient? Explain.

5 Why was the compact fluorescent light bulb developed? What impact does it have on the environment?

6 How might information about a light bulb's energy efficiency influence decisions about technology?

7 Why is a light bulb considered an example of technology?

S.T.E.M. LAB DIRECTED *Inquiry* **AND** GUIDED *Inquiry*

Investigate Digital Information (GENERAL)

Student pairs
45 minutes

MATERIALS

For each pair
- paper, graphing (4 sheets)
- paper, plain (2 sheets)
- pens, black ink (2)

My Notes

LAB RATINGS

LESS ⟷ MORE

Teacher Prep — 1
Student Setup — 1
Cleanup — 1

TEACHER NOTES

In this activity, students will create black and white images on graph paper and digitize them using 1s and 0s. Students will then exchange digital codes with their partners, who will reconstitute them as images. Students should not observe their partners' images in advance; they should attempt to reproduce the images using the digital information alone.

Tip This activity should help students understand how a technology may lead to the development of new systems and products.

Student Tip Not all electronic devices are digital. "Digital" refers to a way of storing information.

Skills Focus Interpreting Data, Applying Concepts

MODIFICATION FOR INDEPENDENT *Inquiry*

Have student pairs develop their own procedures for transmitting information digitally. Students may choose to transmit text or images, either by recording digital code on paper or by saying the digital code aloud. Remind students that digital information is stored using only 1s and 0s. Once they have completed the activity, have student pairs share the methods they used with the class.

S.T.E.M. Lab continued

Answer Key for DIRECTED Inquiry

ANALYZE THE RESULTS

6. Sample answer: I used the digital code to determine which squares in the grid should be black and which should be white. I followed the digits in order from the top left to the bottom right.
7. When an image is saved on a computer, the information is stored as a series of 1s and 0s, just as we used 1s and 0s to record our image on paper.
   Teacher prompt A computer stores information digitally. How is this similar to the way you recorded information?
8. Sample answer: I reproduced one of the rows incorrectly because I misread the order of the digits.

DRAW CONCLUSIONS

9. Sample answer: Digital technology was developed to improve the way information is stored.
   Teacher prompt Does this technology meet a need? Does it improve upon existing technology?
10. Because of digital technology, many new electronic devices store information digitally. For example, a digital camera stores images digitally and not on film.
    Teacher prompt How have certain electronics changed since digital technology was developed? What devices in your home use digital technology?

Connect TO THE ESSENTIAL QUESTION

11. Sample answer: Digital technology has made it easier to share media, such as pictures and music. Now we can share media with friends online instead of in person.
    Teacher prompt Do you ever use digital technology to interact with your family and friends? Are there any problems related to digital technology? Are there any laws regulating its use?

Answer Key for GUIDED Inquiry

DEVELOP A PLAN

4. Accept all reasonable answers.

ANALYZE THE RESULTS

7. Sample answer: I used the digital code to determine which squares in the grid should be black and which should be white. I followed the digits in order from the top left to the bottom right.
8. When an image is saved on a computer, the information is stored as a series of 1s and 0s, just as we used 1s and 0s to record our image on paper.
   Teacher prompt A computer stores information digitally. How is this similar to the way you recorded information?

S.T.E.M. Lab continued

9. Sample answer: I reproduced one of the rows incorrectly because I misread the order of the digits.

DRAW CONCLUSIONS

10. Sample answer: Digital technology was developed to improve the way information is stored.
Teacher prompt Does this technology meet a need? Does it improve upon existing technology?

11. Because of digital technology, many new electronic devices store information digitally. For example, a digital camera stores images digitally and not on film.
Teacher prompt How have certain electronics changed since digital technology was developed? What devices in your home use digital technology?

Connect TO THE ESSENTIAL QUESTION

12. Sample answer: Digital technology has made it easier to share media, such as pictures and music. Now we can share media with friends online instead of in person.
Teacher prompt Do you ever use digital technology to interact with your family and friends? Are there any problems or issues related to digital technology? Are there any laws regulating its use?

Name ______________________ Class ______________ Date ______________

S.T.E.M. LAB DIRECTED *Inquiry*

Investigate Digital Information

In this lab, you will create a black and white image on graph paper and digitize it using 1s and 0s. Then you will send your digital information to a partner who will reproduce the image.

OBJECTIVES

- Identify reasons technology is developed.
- Explain how technology can lead to the development of new technology.

MATERIALS

For each pair
- paper, graphing (4 sheets)
- paper, plain (2 sheets)
- pens, black ink (2)

ASK A QUESTION

1. In this lab, you will investigate the following question: How is information digitally stored and transmitted? Discuss your ideas about this with your partner.

MAKE OBSERVATIONS

2. Obtain a piece of graphing paper and a black pen.
3. Using the black pen, fill in some of the squares of the grid to create a picture or pattern.
4. Record the digital code of your image on plain paper by using 0 for every blank square and 1 for every filled-in square. Write the digits in the order that the squares appear on your grid, starting from the upper left-hand corner. Start a new row of digits for every new row of squares in your picture.
5. Exchange your digital code with a partner who has not seen your picture. Use your partner's code to restore your partner's image on a new piece of graph paper.

ANALYZE THE RESULTS

6. **Describing Methods** How were you able to reproduce your partner's picture?

____

____

____

____

____

S.T.E.M. Lab continued

7 **Applying Concepts** How is this activity similar to saving an image on a computer?

____

____

____

____

8 **Identifying Constraints** Was there any evidence of human error in your investigation? Explain.

____

____

____

____

DRAW CONCLUSIONS

9 **Explaining Events** Why was digital technology developed?

____

____

____

____

____

10 **Applying Concepts** How has digital technology led to the development of new technology? Give an example.

____

____

____

____

____

S.T.E.M. Lab continued

Connect TO THE ESSENTIAL QUESTION

11 **Describing Costs and Benefits** How has digital technology changed our society? Consider social, political, and economic changes.

____

____

____

____

____

____

Name ______________________ Class ______________ Date ______________

S.T.E.M. LAB GUIDED *Inquiry*

Investigate Digital Information

In this lab, you will create a black and white image on graph paper and digitize it using 1s and 0s. Then you will send your digital information to a partner who will reproduce the image.

OBJECTIVES

- Identify reasons technology is developed.
- Explain how technology can lead to the development of new technology.

MATERIALS

For each pair

- paper, graphing (4 sheets)
- paper, plain (2 sheets)
- pens, black ink (2)

ASK A QUESTION

1. In this lab, you will investigate the following question: How is information digitally stored and transmitted? Discuss your ideas with your partner.

DEVELOP A PLAN

2. Obtain a piece of graphing paper and a black pen.
3. Using the black pen, fill in some of the squares of the grid to create a picture or pattern.
4. Devise a procedure that will allow you to record your image on a blank piece of paper using only 1s and 0s.

____

____

____

____

____

____

____

____

5. With your teacher's permission, carry out your procedure and digitize your image.
6. Exchange the digitized code for your image with your partner who has not seen your picture. Use your partner's code to restore your partner's image on a new piece of graph paper.

Name ______________________ Class ______________ Date ________________

S.T.E.M. Lab continued

ANALYZE THE RESULTS

7. **Describing Methods** How were you able to reproduce your partner's picture?

____

____

____

____

____

8. **Applying Concepts** How is this activity similar to saving an image on a computer?

____

____

____

____

9. **Identifying Constraints** Was there any evidence of human error in your investigation? Explain.

____

____

____

____

DRAW CONCLUSIONS

⑩ **Explaining Events** Why was digital technology developed?

⑪ **Applying Concepts** How has digital technology led to the development of new technology? Give an example.

Connect TO THE ESSENTIAL QUESTION

⑫ **Describing Costs and Benefits** How has digital technology changed our society? Consider social, political, and economic changes.